I0409748

# FOOD FOR THOUGHT: EFFORTS TO DEFEND THE NATION'S AGRICULTURE AND FOOD

## HEARING

BEFORE THE

## SUBCOMMITTEE ON EMERGENCY PREPAREDNESS, RESPONSE, AND COMMUNICATIONS

OF THE

## COMMITTEE ON HOMELAND SECURITY HOUSE OF REPRESENTATIVES

ONE HUNDRED FOURTEENTH CONGRESS

SECOND SESSION

FEBRUARY 26, 2016

## Serial No. 114–56

Printed for the use of the Committee on Homeland Security

Available via the World Wide Web: http://www.gpo.gov/fdsys/

U.S. GOVERNMENT PUBLISHING OFFICE

21–528 PDF

WASHINGTON : 2016

For sale by the Superintendent of Documents, U.S. Government Publishing Office
Internet: bookstore.gpo.gov  Phone: toll free (866) 512–1800; DC area (202) 512–1800
Fax: (202) 512–2104  Mail: Stop IDCC, Washington, DC 20402–0001

## COMMITTEE ON HOMELAND SECURITY

MICHAEL T. MCCAUL, Texas, *Chairman*

LAMAR SMITH, Texas
PETER T. KING, New York
MIKE ROGERS, Alabama
CANDICE S. MILLER, Michigan, *Vice Chair*
JEFF DUNCAN, South Carolina
TOM MARINO, Pennsylvania
LOU BARLETTA, Pennsylvania
SCOTT PERRY, Pennsylvania
CURT CLAWSON, Florida
JOHN KATKO, New York
WILL HURD, Texas
EARL L. "BUDDY" CARTER, Georgia
MARK WALKER, North Carolina
BARRY LOUDERMILK, Georgia
MARTHA MCSALLY, Arizona
JOHN RATCLIFFE, Texas
DANIEL M. DONOVAN, JR., New York

BENNIE G. THOMPSON, Mississippi
LORETTA SANCHEZ, California
SHEILA JACKSON LEE, Texas
JAMES R. LANGEVIN, Rhode Island
BRIAN HIGGINS, New York
CEDRIC L. RICHMOND, Louisiana
WILLIAM R. KEATING, Massachusetts
DONALD M. PAYNE, JR., New Jersey
FILEMON VELA, Texas
BONNIE WATSON COLEMAN, New Jersey
KATHLEEN M. RICE, New York
NORMA J. TORRES, California

BRENDAN P. SHIELDS, *Staff Director*
JOAN V. O'HARA, *General Counsel*
MICHAEL S. TWINCHEK, *Chief Clerk*
I. LANIER AVANT, *Minority Staff Director*

———

## SUBCOMMITTEE ON EMERGENCY PREPAREDNESS, RESPONSE, AND COMMUNICATIONS

MARTHA MCSALLY, Arizona, *Chairman*

TOM MARINO, Pennsylvania
MARK WALKER, North Carolina
BARRY LOUDERMILK, Georgia
DANIEL M. DONOVAN, JR., New York
MICHAEL T. MCCAUL, Texas *(ex officio)*

DONALD M. PAYNE, JR., New Jersey
BONNIE WATSON COLEMAN, New Jersey
KATHLEEN M. RICE, New York
BENNIE G. THOMPSON, Mississippi *(ex officio)*

KERRY A. KINIRONS, *Subcommittee Staff Director*
JOHN DICKHAUS, *Subcommittee Clerk*
MOIRA BERGIN, *Minority Subcommittee Staff Director*

# CONTENTS

# FOOD FOR THOUGHT: EFFORTS TO DEFEND THE NATION'S AGRICULTURE AND FOOD

---

**Friday, February 26, 2016**

U.S. HOUSE OF REPRESENTATIVES,
SUBCOMMITTEE ON EMERGENCY PREPAREDNESS,
RESPONSE, AND COMMUNICATIONS,
COMMITTEE ON HOMELAND SECURITY,
*Washington, DC.*

The subcommittee met, pursuant to call, at 10:13 a.m., in Room 311, Cannon House Office Building, Hon. Martha McSally [Chairman of the subcommittee] presiding.

Present: Representatives McSally, Walker, Loudermilk, Donovan, Payne, and Watson Coleman.

Ms. MCSALLY. The Subcommittee on Emergency Preparedness Response and Communications will come to order.

The subcommittee's meeting today to receive testimony regarding the efforts to defend our Nation's food and agriculture sector. I now recognize myself for an opening statement.

Let me first say this is my last subcommittee hearing that I will be chairing. Technically, I have actually handed over the gavel to my good colleague here, Mr. Donovan from New York, but since we had planned this hearing, we decided to do our change of command ceremony at the end of the hearing. So, it is an absolute honor to have been chairing this subcommittee and working with my colleagues and my Ranking Member, Mr. Payne. I will be remaining on the subcommittee, but I will be chairing the Border and Maritime Subcommittee now, which is, obviously, quite important for my district, and looking forward to continued leadership opportunities.

Anyway back to the topic at hand. Throughout this Congress, the Subcommittee on Emergency Preparedness, Response, and Communications has taken a deep dive into the world of biological terrorism. We have held hearings to assess the biological threat, understand the scope of the biodefense problem, and examine Federal programs aimed at tackling some of the biodefense challenges. Our oversight thus far has primarily been on the human impacts of biological terrorism.

Today we are going to take a different perspective, and look at the impacts to the Nation from a terrorist attack on, or natural disruption of, our agricultural or food systems. An agroterrorism attack would impact the most basic of human needs: The food we eat. Furthermore, the food and agricultural sector is critically important to our Nation's economy. U.S. food and agriculture accounts for roughly one-fifth of the Nation's economic activity, contributing

$835 billion to the U.S. gross domestic product in 2014, and is responsible for 1 out of every 12 U.S. jobs.

In my home State of Arizona, ranching and agriculture contributes around $10 billion a year to the State's economy. An intentional attack on, or natural disruption of, U.S. agriculture, or food, therefore, would present a serious threat to this Nation and cause major economic damage on a number of levels.

There will be costs related to containing disease, and destruction of livestock, compensating farmers for loss of agriculture commodities, and losses in other related industries, and trade embargoes imposed by other nations.

Intelligence indicates that terrorists have discussed vulnerabilities in various components of this sector. Food and agriculture is an attractive target to terrorists, because many agents are easy to obtain; minimal technology is required to execute an attack, and our food travels across the country and world quickly and efficiently.

Furthermore, even if there are few human casualties, an agroterrorism attack would also undermine public confidence in the Government, increasing general concerns about the safety of our food supply, as well as the effectiveness of biological defense planning. This goes to the heart of what we know groups like ISIS are trying to do, terrorize by all means possible.

We all need to look at the impacts of the highly pathogenic avian influenza, or HPAI, a natural event to see how devastating an intentional act against our food or agriculture could be. Last year's outbreak of HPAI was the largest animal health incident in U.S. history, resulting in over $3 billion in economic losses, and the slaughtering of 48 million birds to stem the spread of the disease. Eighteen trading partners banned all imports of U.S. poultry and products, and an additional 28 trading partners imposed partial bans. This outbreak, and its rapid farm-to-farm spread, highlighted the challenge the sector faces related to effective biosecurity, especially during a large-scale response.

We must ensure we are able to assess our level of preparedness for any type of major disruption to U.S. food or agriculture. Our goal today is to gain a better understanding of what Government, along with academia and the private sector, are doing to reduce vulnerabilities of the food and agriculture sector to a terrorist attack.

We hope to gain a better understanding of the scope of the problem, and identify ways in which we, as Members of Congress focused on Homeland Security issues, can help prevent attacks, and improve our readiness and our ability to respond.

I hope to hear about information sharing with the Government. Is food and agriculture engaged in our process, including things like the fusion centers? Are you getting the threat and risk information that you need? I also want to understand your connectedness to the human health side of things. Are our current biosurveillance systems integrating the human, animal, and plant data to form one true, "One Health" picture?

With that, I welcome our witnesses, and I look forward to your testimony.

[The statement of Chairman McSally follows:]

## STATEMENT OF CHAIRMAN MARTHA MCSALLY

### FEBRUARY 26, 2016

Throughout this Congress, the Subcommittee on Emergency Preparedness, Response, and Communications has taken a deep dive into the world of biological terrorism. We have held hearings to assess the biological threat, understand the scope of the biodefense problem, and examine Federal programs aimed at tackling some of the biodefense challenges.

Our oversight thus far has primarily been on the human impacts of biological terrorism. Today we are going to take a different perspective and look at the impacts to the Nation from a terrorist attack on, or natural disruption of, our agricultural or food systems.

An agroterrorism attack would impact the most basic of human needs—the food we eat. Furthermore, the food and agriculture sector is critically important to our nation's economy. U.S. food and agriculture accounts for roughly one-fifth of the Nation's economic activity, contributed $835 billion to the U.S. gross domestic product (GDP) in 2014, and is responsible for one out of every 12 U.S. jobs. In my home State of Arizona, ranching and agriculture contributes around $10 billion a year to the State's economy.

An intentional attack or natural disruption of U.S. agriculture or food, therefore, would present a serious threat to this Nation and cause major economic damages on a number of levels. There will be costs related to containing disease and destruction of livestock, compensating farmers for loss of agricultural commodities and losses in other related industries, and trade embargoes imposed by other nations.

Intelligence indicates that terrorists have discussed vulnerabilities in various components of the sector. Food and agriculture is an attractive target to terrorists because many agents are easy to obtain, minimal technology is required to execute an attack, and our food travels across the country and world quickly and efficiently.

Furthermore, even if there are few human casualties, an agroterrorism attack would also undermine public confidence in Government, increasing general concerns about the safety of our food supply as well as the effectiveness of biological defense planning. This goes to the heart of what we know groups like ISIS are trying to do—terrorize by any means possible.

We need only look at the impacts of highly pathogenic avian influenza (HPAI), a natural event, to see how devastating an intentional act against our food or agriculture could be. Last year's outbreak of HPAI was the largest animal health incident in U.S. history, resulting in over $3 billion in economic losses and the slaughtering of 48 million birds to stem the spread of disease. Eighteen trading partners banned all imports of U.S. poultry and products and an additional 28 trading partners imposed partial bans.

This outbreak and its rapid farm-to-farm spread highlighted the challenges the sector faces related to effective biosecurity, especially during a large-scale response.

We must ensure we are able to assess our level of preparedness for any type of major disruption to U.S. food or agriculture. Our goal today is to gain a better understanding of what Government, along with academia and the private sector, are doing to reduce vulnerabilities of the food and agricultural sector to a terrorist attack.

We hope to gain a better understanding of the scope of the problem, and identify ways in which we as Members of Congress focused on homeland security issues can help prevent attacks and improve our readiness and ability to respond.

I hope to hear about information sharing with Government. Is food and agriculture engaged in our processes including fusion centers? Are you getting the threat and risk information you need? I also want to understand your connectedness to the human health side of things—are our current biosurveillance systems integrating the human, animal, and plant data to form a true "One Health" picture?

With that, I welcome our witnesses. I look forward to your testimony.

Ms. MCSALLY. The Chair now recognizes the gentleman from New Jersey, Mr. Payne, for any opening statement he may have.

Mr. PAYNE. Thank you, Madam Chair. Good morning to all here. I would like to thank subcommittee Chair, Ms. McSally, for holding today's chair. Madam Chair, I wish you the best of luck as you take over the Subcommittee on Border and Maritime Security.

Ms. MCSALLY. Thank you.

Mr. PAYNE. Biological threats are evolving. As these threats evolve, so does our perspective about how we can best protect against the damage that they can inflict. This subcommittee has historically focused on the human health impact of the biological threats. I am pleased that we are expanding the scope of our oversight to include the impact to U.S. agriculture and food supply.

I represent the 10th Congressional District of the State of New Jersey. Now, my district is not known for its rolling fields of corn, hog pens or open cattle ranges. It is, however, home of the Port of Newark, and Newark Liberty International Airport. Customs and Border Protection agriculture specialists at the airport clear up to 20,000 passengers every day. At Port Newark, one of the busiest ports on the East Coast, specialists inspect imported food, items, marble slabs, tiles, and wood-packing material, all of which can carry insects and other snails that could harm our domestic agriculture. Yet, just this week, I heard the CPB employees in my district about insufficient agriculture specialist staffing.

The Port of Newark and Newark International Airport are top performing ports, with top interception numbers and several first-in-the-Nation insect finds. But I am concerned that unless the staffing challenges are resolved, there is a risk that a new foreign insect could go undetected and do harm to the agriculture industry and the safety of the food supply.

Although I recognize that we may not be able to stop every dangerous insect or pathogen from entering our borders, we must be vigilant. With that said, I also recognize that there are domestic risks to agriculture—the agriculture industry and the food supply related to natural disasters and emerging disease, diseasing and bad actors.

Last year, for example, an avian influenza outbreak was responsible for nearly $400 million in losses to the egg and poultry industry, and consumers paid the price at the grocery store. Although the Avian influenza was a naturally-occurring event, the financial losses sustained served as a sobering example of the economic damage that a significant agriculture incident could inflict.

The food and agricultural industry is valued at nearly $1 trillion in the United States, and its criticality to the American people is without question. That is why the Federal Government has designated the food and agriculture sector a critical infrastructure sector since 2003.

Although there are multiple efforts to enhance the security of the agriculture industry underway at the Federal and State level, as well as within industry, significant challenges remain. For example, earlier this month, this subcommittee held a hearing on the Department of Homeland Security's struggle to achieve a National biosurveillance capability to collect and analyze biosurveillance data related to human health, animal health, and plant health.

Unfortunately, this DHS National Biosurveillance Integration Center has struggled to effectively execute its mission for nearly a decade to the detriment of efforts to improve the agricultural biosurveillance capabilities. I will be interested to know what, if any, recommendations the witnesses have to improve the National biosurveillance capability in that regard.

Additionally, I will be interested in understanding how information related to emerging diseases, emergency planning for natural disasters, and terrorist threats is shared with stakeholders in the agricultural industry, and whether the information is actionable.

Finally, I am eager to learn from our witnesses how the private sector, educational institutions, and non-Government entities can play an active role in developing and enhancing biosecurity protocols for the agriculture industry as a whole.

I thank the witnesses for being here today, and I look forward to hearing your testimony. Madam Chair, with that, I yield back the balance of my time.

[The statement of Ranking Member Payne follows:]

STATEMENT OF RANKING MEMBER DONALD M. PAYNE JR.

FEBRUARY 26, 2016

Biological threats are evolving. As these threats evolve, so does our perspective about how we can best protect against the damage they can inflict. This subcommittee has historically focused on the human health impact of the biological threats. I am pleased that we are expanding the scope of our oversight to include the impact to U.S. agriculture and food supply.

I represent the 10th Congressional district of New Jersey. My district is not known for its rolling fields of corn, hog pens, or open cattle ranges. It is, however, home of the Port of Newark and Newark Liberty International Airport.

Customs and Border Protection Agriculture Specialists at that airport clear up to 20,000 passengers every day. At Port Newark—one of the busiest ports on the East Coast—specialists inspect imported food items, marble slabs, tiles, and wood-packing material, all of which can carry insects or other snails that could harm domestic agriculture.

Yet, just this week, I heard from CBP employees in my district about insufficient Agriculture Specialist staffing. The Port of Newark and Newark Liberty International Airport are top performing ports, with top interception numbers, and several "First-in-Nation" insect finds.

But I am concerned that unless the staffing challenges are resolved, there's a risk that a new foreign insect could go undetected and do harm to the agriculture industry and the safety of the food supply. Although I recognize that we may not be able to stop every dangerous insect or pathogen from entering our borders, we must be vigilant.

With that said, I also recognize that there are domestic risks to the agriculture industry and food supply—related to natural disasters, emerging disease, and bad actors. Last year, for example, an avian influenza outbreak was responsible for nearly $400 million in losses to the egg and poultry industry.

And consumers paid the price at the grocery store. Although avian influenza was a naturally-occurring event, the financial losses sustained served as a sobering example of the economic damage that a significant agricultural incident could inflict.

The food and agriculture industry is valued at nearly a trillion dollars in the United States, and its criticality to the American people is without question. That is why the Federal Government has designated the Food and Agriculture Sector a critical infrastructure sector since 2003. Although there are multiple efforts to enhance the security of the agriculture industry underway at the Federal and State level, as well as within industry, significant challenges remain.

For example, earlier this month, this subcommittee held a hearing on the Department of Homeland Security's struggle to achieve a National biosurveillance capability to collect and analyze biosurveillance data related to human health, animal health, and plant health. Unfortunately, this DHS's National Biosurveillance Integration Center has struggled to effectively execute its mission for nearly a decade, to the detriment of efforts to improve agriculture biosurveillance capabilities. I will be interested to know what, if any, recommendations the witnesses have to improve the National biosurveillance capability in that regard.

Additionally, I will be interested in understanding how information related to emerging diseases, emergency planning for natural disasters, and terrorist threats is shared with stakeholders in the agriculture industry and whether the information is actionable.

Finally, I am eager to learn from our witnesses how the private sector, educational institutions, and other non-Government entities can play an active role in developing and enhancing biosecurity protocols for the agriculture industry as a whole.

Ms. McSALLY. Thank you, Ranking Member Payne. Other Members of the subcommittee are reminded that opening statements may be submitted for the record.

[The statement of Ranking Member Thompson follows:]

STATEMENT OF RANKING MEMBER BENNIE G. THOMPSON

FEBRUARY 26, 2016

Before we begin, I would like to thank all of the witnesses for being here today, especially Professor Brian Williams from Mississippi State University. Mr. Williams is a professor at Mississippi State's College of Agriculture Economics and will provide important insight into the economic effects of an agro-event—whether man-made or naturally-occurring. I would like to thank him for making the trip to Washington to share his important insights with us today. I represent a district in Mississippi where agriculture is the No. 1 source of income.

From catfish and poultry to hogs and rice, agriculture accounts for $10.6 billion in annual revenue—or over 15 percent—of the State's income. Any significant disruption to the agriculture industry there—whether at the hands of terrorist actors, emerging diseases, or natural disasters—would have devastating rippling effects throughout the State and the Nation. That is why I have worked hard to advance programs that improve the National capability to prevent—and mitigate the impact of—biological events affecting agriculture and improve resiliency within the industry.

I am interested in hearing our witness' assessment of Federal efforts to protect the Nation's food supply and to better understand the risks to our agriculture sector. Late last year, the Blue Ribbon Study Panel on Biodefense released a report that identified capability gaps across the National biodefense enterprise. The Panel's report focused on biodefense efforts associated with protecting human health. It also addressed bio-threats to agriculture.

An important recommendation from the report called for enhanced surveillance and detection of biological threats to animal health. This would be achieved through the establishment of a "Nationally notifiable animal disease system" modeled after the existing system for identifying human disease outbreaks.

Too often, we find that information sharing does not take place across units of Government and the private sector. Hopefully, our witnesses can shed light on whether the Federal Government is doing enough to identify international threats to the agriculture industry. I believe these actions must be timely and fact-based to protect domestic livestock and crops. Domestically, we should examine whether animal disease reporting requirements ensure that emerging diseases are identified. That information is central to the ability of health and safety officials to contain an outbreak.

The U.S. Department of Agriculture has proposed the creation of a National List of Reportable Animal Diseases. I would be interested to hear whether the existence of such a list would be helpful to agricultural stakeholders and whether it could be designed in a way where States and other owners of disease information could willingly and comfortably report disease incidence?

Moreover, I want to understand the extent to which the agriculture industry has been included in emergency planning activities so that it is resilient in the wake of a natural disaster. Now that NBAF has received its construction funding, I want to learn about the research that will be conducted on biological threats to livestock and animal diseases that can impact human health. To that end, I would like to learn more about Kansas State's partnership with NBAF, the research that will be pursued, and how its work will advance National agro-defense capabilities.

Ms. McSALLY. We are pleased to have a very distinguished panel before us today on this important topic. Dr. Doug Meckes is the North Carolina State veterinarian, a position he has held since 2014. Prior to that, Dr. Meckes served as the branch chief for Food, Agriculture, and Veterinary Defense at the U.S. Department of Homeland Security, where he provided oversight and management of the Department's implementation of Homeland Security Presidential Directive–9, Defense of the United States Agriculture and Food, Integrating the efforts of other DHS components, and coordinating those efforts with appropriate Federal departments and agencies, Tribal, State, and local governments, and the private sector.

Dr. Tammy Beckham is dean of the College of Veterinary Medicine at Kansas State University, a position she assumed in August 2015. Prior to her current position, Dr. Beckham served as the director of the Institute for Infectious Animal Diseases, or IIAD, a Department of Homeland Security Center of Excellence in College Station, Texas, where she led the IIAD's effort to perform research and develop products to defend the Nation from high consequence, foreign, animal, emerging, and zoonotic diseases. Did I say that right?

Dr. BECKHAM. Excellent.

Ms. McSALLY. I was a premed biology major in college. My professors would not be proud of me.

Anyway, Dr. Beckham also served as director of the Texas A&M Veterinary Medical Diagnostic laboratory, where she provided leadership for its two full-service laboratories and two poultry laboratories, and directs one of the highest-volume animal diagnostic labs in the country.

Previously, Dr. Beckham was director of the Foreign Animal Disease Diagnostic laboratory, part of the U.S. Department of Agriculture's Plum Island Animal Disease Center in New York. Her responsibilities included managing the diagnosis of animal diseases; overseeing diagnostic test development for a Nation-wide animal health diagnostic system; and coordinating efforts with the Department of Homeland Security and National Animal Health Laboratory Network and other entities.

Mr. Bobby Acord has been a consultant for the National Pork Producers Council since 2004. Prior to that, Mr. Acord served as administrator for the U.S. Department of Agriculture's Animal and Plant Health Inspection Services from 2001 to 2004. As APHIS's— is that how you pronounce it—administrator, Mr. Acord was responsible for protecting U.S. agricultural health from exotic pests and diseases, administering the Animal Welfare Act, and carrying out wildlife damage management activities. Mr. Acord served as APHIS's associate administrator from 1999 to 2001. Prior to that, he served nearly a decade as deputy administrator for APHIS's wildlife services program.

Dr. Brian Williams is an assistant extension professor at the Mississippi State University, Department of Agricultural Economics. Dr. Williams focuses on the primary areas of commodity marketing, farm management, production economics, and agricultural policy. Since joining the department, he has served as a member of the Mississippi University disaster response team, where he has focused on assessing damage to the agricultural academic sector after natural disasters. The witnesses' full written statements will appear in the record.

The Chair now recognizes Dr. Meckes for 5 minutes.

## STATEMENT OF R. DOUGLAS MECKES, D.V.M., STATE VETERI-NARIAN, NORTH CAROLINA DEPARTMENT OF AGRICULTURE AND CONSUMER SERVICES, VETERINARY DIVISION

Dr. MECKES. Red light. Chairman McSally, Ranking Member Payne, Members of the House Subcommittee on Preparedness, Response, and Communications. My name is Doug Meckes, and I am the State veterinarian and the director of the veterinary division in North Carolina's Department of Agriculture and consumer services. The division serves the poultry industry, the livestock industry, and manages and operates 4 veterinary diagnostic laboratories in North Carolina.

Thank you for the opportunity to speak today about North Carolina's on-going efforts to prepare for, respond to, and communicate with stakeholders during agricultural emergencies.

North Carolina and Georgia's robust agriculture and agribusiness industry, which contributes nearly $80 billion annually to North Carolina's economy. Sixty-seven percent of that figure is associated animal agriculture. The industry accounts for 17 percent of State's income and employs 16 percent of the workforce.

Chairman McSally and Ranking Member Payne have spoken knowledgeably about the food and ag sectors writ large, and I will not speak to that. But mindful of the contributions of the food and ag sector to the Nation, in January 2004, Homeland Security Presidential Directive–9 was released and established a National policy to defend agriculture food and food systems against terrorist attacks, major disasters, and other emergencies.

Included in HSPD–9 were 18 line items which provide guidance to address then-identified gaps in our Nation's ability to identify agriculture and food. Twelve years, later, gaps remain in our efforts to fulfill the HSPD–9 directives.

I will speak to North Carolina's concerns over 3 of those gaps today. Federal, State, and local responses capabilities, availability of vaccine for foot-and-mouth disease, and the National Animal Health Laboratory Network resources. Line item 14 of HSPD–9 directs participating departments and agencies to ensure that the Federal, State, and local response capabilities are adequate to respond effectively to a terrorist attack, to major disease outbreaks, or other disaster.

Even before HSPD–9, my predecessors in North Carolina recognized the need for such capability. That need was precipitated by a series of events in the State, in the Nation, and internationally. In September 1999, Hurricane Floyd made landfall in North Carolina, and that resulted in $813 million in agriculture losses.

In February 2001, an outbreak of foot-and-mouth disease in the United Kingdom caused a crisis in agriculture and tourism.

Finally, 9/11 brought new concerns of attacks on our agriculture and food systems. The likelihood of agroterrorism, the deliberate introduction of animal plant disease for the purpose of generating fear, and causing economic losses, and undermining social stability took on new meaning.

In the midst of these events, North Carolina's veterinary division launched an effort to meet the challenges of agriculture and food in the 21st Century. As a result, the emergency programs division was created within the department to reduce the vulnerability, minimize the impact of any natural or man-made disaster, disease, or terrorist attack, and to facilitate a rapid return to normalcy.

Today, the emergency programs division within North Carolina has reached maturity and has more than fulfilled its all hazards response mission. Development of this capability has been funded by State and various Federal grants: $18 million in State funds, $7.3 million in Federal funds, a relatively small investment over the years.

Consider what similar investments might have meant to States so profoundly affected by HPAI. Iowa and Minnesota experienced $1.6–1.8 billion in economic losses as a result of HPAI on 180 premises.

Continued Federal, State funding will be necessary to maintain current capability to develop new capability to train, to exercise, to replace equipment as needed. Unfortunately, funding for North Carolina's emergency program division continues to decline, and places the State's preparedness and response capability at risk.

North Carolina's second concern, line item 18(a) of HSPD–9, speaks to the necessity of developing a National Veterinary Stockpile, containing sufficient amounts of animal vaccine antivirals, therapeutic products to appropriately respond to the most damaging animal diseases.

Foremost in the minds with States with significant animal agriculture production is the possibility of a foot-and-mouth disease outbreak. Certainly, that is the case in North Carolina, home to 9 million hogs. The size, the structure, the efficiency, and the extensive movement inherent in U.S. livestock industry, will present unprecedented challenges in the event of an FMD outbreak. Control of such an outbreak in livestock-dense areas will require tens of millions of doses of foot-and-mouth disease vaccine.

However, there are not tens of millions of doses of foot-and-mouth disease available, not anywhere in the world, because there is no excess production capacity. Current production meets daily needs, and there is no excess capacity. The reality has been evident since 2004, when the National Veterinary Stockpile was created, but there has never been sufficient funding to stockpile foot-and-mouth disease vaccines.

FMD remains North Carolina's animal agriculture's greatest threat. The pork industry, the economy, communities, businesses, and families in North Carolina would be devastated by a foot-and-mouth disease outbreak. A cooperative collaborative effort, which includes all stakeholders must be initiated to develop and implement a plan for establishing an effective FMD stockpile.

North Carolina's third concern is veterinary diagnostic laboratory capability. Line item 8, HSPD–9, directs departments and agencies to develop a Nation-wide laboratory network for food, veterinary, plant, health, and water resources that integrate Federal and State laboratory resources. The National Animal Health Laboratory Network was created as a result of this directive, and is now a part of the Nation-wide strategy to coordinate the work of all organizations providing animal disease surveillance and testing services.

North Carolina's veterinary diagnostic laboratory system is a part of NAHLN, effectively surveils for and diagnoses animals' zoonotic diseases every day. However, State and Federal support of and full funding for the Nation's NAHLN laboratory system are necessary to optimize capability.

The absence of full funding for the NAHLN was recently noted in the bipartisan report of the Blue Ribbon Study Panel on Bio-defense, which stated: "The NAHLN has struggled to maintain even $10 million of annual funding. Its appropriations cut over the years to pay for other programs. As a result, laboratories are un-able to meet the threat and at times eliminate positions and test-ing capacity for foreign animal diseases."

After struggling for years to obtain sufficient funding, Congress, in 2014, authorized the specific funding line for NAHLN at $15 million. NAHLN must be funded at this authorized level in order to meet the need.

Thank you for the opportunity to speak today on behalf of North Carolina, about issues of concern related to the defense in food and agriculture. I am happy to address any questions you may have.

[The prepared statement of Dr. Meckes follows:]

PREPARED STATEMENT OF R. DOUGLAS MECKES

FEBRUARY 26, 2016

Chairman Donovan, Ranking Member Payne, and Members of the House Sub-committee on Preparedness, Response, and Communications, my name is Doug Meckes and I am the State veterinarian and the director of the Veterinary Division in North Carolina's Department of Agriculture and Consumer Services. The division includes 150 employees that serve the poultry industry and the livestock industry, that manage and operate the State's 4 veterinary diagnostic laboratories, and that are charged with oversight of 866 kennels and shelters caring for companion ani-mals in North Carolina. Thank you for the opportunity to speak about matters of concern in North Carolina's on-going efforts to prepare for, respond to, and commu-nicate with stakeholders during agricultural emergencies.

North Carolina enjoys a robust agriculture and agribusiness industry which con-tributes nearly $80 billion on an annual basis to North Carolina's economy; 66% of that figure is associated with animal agriculture and North Carolina ranks second in hog production and third in overall poultry production in the Nation. On an an-nual basis, the industry accounts for 17% of the State's income and employs 16% of the workforce. North Carolina's agriculture/agribusiness industry is part of the greater Food and Agriculture Sector (FA Sector), designated by Homeland Security a critical infrastructure sector in 2003 thus recognizing its significant contribution to National security and the economy.[1]

The FA Sector is composed of complex production, processing, and delivery sys-tems and has the capacity to feed people and animals both within and beyond the boundaries of the United States. These food and agriculture systems are almost en-tirely under private ownership, operate in highly competitive global markets, strive to operate in harmony with the environment, and provide economic opportunities and an improved quality of life for American citizens and others world-wide. The FA Sector accounts for roughly one-fifth of the Nation's economic activity. In 2012, total agricultural product sales amounted to $400 billion, with crops and livestock each accounting for roughly half of those sales. One-fifth of U.S. agricultural produc-tion is exported, generating $144.1 billion in 2013, creating a positive trade balance of roughly $40 billion, and thereby fueling the U.S. economy.[2]

In January 2004, Homeland Security Presidential Directive–9 (HSPD–9) "estab-lished a National policy to defend the agriculture system against terrorists' attack, major disasters, and other emergencies." Included in HSPD–9 were 18 "line items" which provide guidance to address then-identified gaps in the Nation's ability to de-fend agriculture and food. Twelve years later, progress has been made in addressing some of the gaps including a star in the crown of agriculture and food defense: Line Item 24 in HSPD–9—the design and initiation of construction for "safe, secure, and state-of-the-art agriculture biocontainment laboratories that research and develop

---

[1] Mike Walden, Reynolds Professor and Extension Economist, NC State University's College of Agriculture and Life Sciences.
[2] Food and Agriculture Sector-Specific Plan (SSP) 2015.

diagnostic capabilities for foreign animal and zoonotic diseases," the National Agro-Biodefense facility in Manhattan, Kansas. This achievement notwithstanding, other gaps in HSPD–9 have not been sufficiently addressed.

In the interest of full disclosure, prior to accepting my position in North Carolina, I was fully engaged in "providing oversight and management of the Department's (DHS's) implementation of HSPD–9" in my role as branch chief, Food, Agriculture and Veterinary Defense Branch of the Office of Health Affairs, Department of Homeland Security. Thus, through my experiences with DHS and now as State veterinarian, I have gained unique insight into what is/should be required at the State level to defend agriculture and food. I will speak to 3 of North Carolina's concerns today: Federal, State, and local response capabilities, availability of vaccine for Foot-and-Mouth disease, and National Animal Health Laboratory Network resources.

Line Item 14 of HSPD–9 directs the participating Departments/Agencies to ensure "that the combined Federal, State, and local response capabilities are adequate to respond quickly and effectively to a terrorist attack, major disease outbreak, or other disaster affecting the National agriculture or food infrastructure." Even before HSPD–9, members of the North Carolina Department of Agriculture and Consumer Services (NCDA&CS), my predecessors, recognized the need for such a capability. Today, as the North Carolina State Veterinarian, I am the fortunate benefactor of their insight, vision, and planning to prepare for and respond to agriculture and food incidents of any magnitude. The need for this capability was precipitated by a series of events in the State, in the Nation, and internationally. In September 1999, Hurricane Floyd made landfall in North Carolina. The hurricane, and associated weather conditions before and after, resulted in the most severe flooding and devastation in North Carolina's history. That flooding resulted in an estimated $813 million in agricultural losses affecting 32,000 farmers. In addition to crop losses, livestock losses—almost 3 million poultry, 28,000 swine, and 600 hundred cattle—created problems associated with disposal of the carcasses of the animals.[3] In February 2001, an outbreak of foot-and-mouth disease in the United Kingdom caused a crisis in British agriculture and tourism. This epizootic saw 2,000 cases of the disease in farms across most of the British countryside. Over 10 million sheep and cattle were depopulated in an eventually successful attempt to halt the disease. By the time that the disease was controlled, in October 2001, the crisis was estimated to have cost the United Kingdom over US$6 billion. Finally, the attacks of 9/11 and the subsequent 2001 anthrax attacks, also known as Amerithrax, brought new concerns of attacks on our agricultural and food systems. The likelihood of "agroterrorism," "the deliberate introduction of an animal or plant disease for the purpose of generating fear, causing economic losses, or undermining social stability," took on new meaning.

In the midst of these events, the director of the Veterinary Division in NCDA&CS took on the task of developing capabilities to better protect North Carolina's animal health and to formulate a plan to meet the challenges of agriculture and food in the 21st Century. The sum of the director's efforts in this regard created the Emergency Programs Division within the Department. The mission of the Division is to: "Reduce the vulnerability and minimize the impact from any natural or man-made disaster, disease outbreak, or terrorist attack for the Department, the people and the agricultural interest of the State and to facilitate a rapid return to normalcy." Obviously, given the possible origins of a disaster, a broad spectrum of multi-hazard events must be considered.

In 2002, the Agricultural Emergency Operations Center (AgEOC) was completed and 4 primary activities were identified:

1. Continuation of the threat assessment and threat reduction efforts within the Department and the agriculture community.

2. Training of AgEOC staff in operations and conduct of exercises for Multi-Hazard events.

3. Completion of the Multi-Hazard Response Plan.

4. Securing adequate funding for the continued development of the Multi-Hazard Threat Database (MHTD), and full implementation of the NC Threat Reduction Plan.

The MHTD built by and for the use of the NCDA&CS, is a collection of both secure and public facing web-based applications. It provides detailed situational awareness in all events; examples would include: Flooding and wind projections during hurricanes for the FA Sector; visualization of disease spread; premises and facility locations for isolation/quarantine within a control area; vehicle routing during disease outbreaks; and food and feed firm's activities during recalls/food illness outbreaks. Additionally, the MHTD facilitates and supports all activities associated

---

[3] North Carolina State Animal Response Team (SART) Animal Burial Guidelines 2003.

with strategic planning, emergency response, incident command structure, and resource management during events. NCDA&CS is currently in the process of developing a 5-year plan to retool and bolster the effectiveness and complete integration of MHTD into the North Carolina FA Sector; the end-product of this effort—a MHTD tool capable of successfully guiding North Carolina through any all-hazards event and returning/restoring the economy, the environment, and the citizens to pre-event status.

Today, the Emergency Programs Division (EP Division) has reached maturity and its sphere of operation is considered All-Hazards in nature; as such, the EP Division is actively engaged in the support of other divisions within the Department, collaborates and coordinates with other departments and agencies across local, State, and Federal government, with industry and academia, and has rendered assistance to other States in a variety of instances. The EP Division's mission and goals are now well-defined.

## MISSION

The NCDA&CS Emergency Programs Division's mission is to reduce the vulnerability to or the impact from, any disaster, disease, or terrorist attack on the agriculture community of North Carolina. The Division serves in a leadership capacity within the Department and works closely with local communities to support agrosecurity, agricultural emergency preparedness and recovery, and rapid response technology efforts. The EP Division establishes public-private partnerships between vital government agencies, industry, and volunteers to carry out this mission.

## GOALS

- Preserve the ability of the N.C. agriculture community to produce stable supplies of food and other agricultural products.
- Diagnose and investigate infectious animal and livestock diseases, intentional plant pest introductions, unauthorized biological control agent releases, and environmental health problems and health hazards in the N.C. agriculture community.
- Provide the full resources of the North Carolina Department of Agriculture & Consumer Services to support the State of North Carolina in any emergency situation.
- Reduce the vulnerability of the staff, vital assets, services, and operations of the North Carolina Department of Agriculture & Consumer Services.
- Reduce the vulnerability of State animal, livestock, plant, crop, and other beneficial organism populations from the effect of a Multi-Hazard emergency event.
- Support the partners and customers of the North Carolina Department of Agriculture & Consumer Services in reducing their vulnerability to and recovery from the effect of a Multi-Hazard emergency event.
- Inform, educate, and empower people to respond to specific agricultural community issues pertaining to a threatened or actual Multi-Hazard emergency event.
- Enforce laws and regulations that protect public, animal, livestock, plant, crop, and other beneficial organism's health and ensure their general safety in case of a Multi-Hazard emergency event.
- Evaluate the effectiveness, accessibility, and quality of departmental and community-based agricultural services available to respond to a Multi-Hazard emergency event.

The measure of success of the EP Division's efforts to accomplish its All-Hazards Response mission is best characterized by the breadth of its activities.

## THE CASTLEBERRY FOOD RECALL IN NORTH CAROLINA

On July 18, 2007, Castleberry's Food Company announced that it was voluntarily recalling several products and working with the U.S. Food and Drug Administration (FDA), the United States Department of Agriculture (USDA), and the Centers for Disease Control and Prevention (CDC) to investigate possible contamination of these products with Clostridium Botulinum, a bacterium which can cause botulism, a life-threatening illness. Upon notification of this recall, NCDA&CS Food and Drug Protection Division and Meat and Poultry Inspection Division jointly initiated response actions on July 20, 2007 and began to monitor the situation. At the time there was little data known about the recall. As the seriousness of the situation became clearer through communications with FDA, NCDA&CS initiated the formation of the Castleberry Recall Incident Management Team (IMT) and activated the Joint Food Emergency Operations Command Center. Food and Drug Protection Division became the multi-agency coordinator for North Carolina food defense agencies and set up the command center at the NCDA&CS Constable Laboratory, in Raleigh, NC.

The director instituted the use of the Incident Command System (ICS) to manage the incident on July 25, 2007 and began development of daily Incident Action Plans. The initial planning process incorporated the Food and Drug Protection Division, Meat and Poultry Inspection Division, Public Affairs Division, Agricultural Statistics Division, and EP Division into the event operations.

The early implementation of the ICS by the NCDA&CS and other State agencies to manage the event was seen by all responding agencies as one of the keys to the overall success of the operation. The activation of the Joint Food Emergency Operations Command Center allowed the various State and local agencies with response authority and capability to act in a uniform and consistent manner, which contributed to the success and positive mission outcomes of the operation. At the end of the recall, over 35,000 cans of product were removed from outlets across North Carolina, more that the total of all products collected by the rest of the United States agencies engaged in the recall.

## EVANS ROAD FIRE

In June of 2008 a wildfire broke out in Eastern North Carolina consuming over 40,000 acres. Utilizing the web-based Emergency Operations Center (WebEOC), EP Division coordinated the NCDA&CS response and support activities for this event. Logistical support was provided in the form of a loan of 320 gallons of fire suppression foam from EP Division's Avian Influenza (AI) response inventory, pumps, and hoses. The Department also provided 2 trucks for dust abatement as well as personnel from Plant Industries Division. Food distribution was also supplied in the form of 2 refrigerated trailers to support food service for the fire fighters.

## TOMATO AND PEPPER SALMONELLA INVESTIGATION

The NCDA&CS Emergency Program Division assisted the Food and Drug Protection Division in its response to a National Salmonella outbreak in various fresh produce products in the late summer 2008. Due to the complexity of the event and potential serious consequences for consumers and producers alike, EP Division assisted in the establishment of a Multi-Agency Joint Operation Center at the Food and Drug Division's Constable Laboratory. Specifically EP Division: Developed and distributed daily Incident Action Plans; refined procedures to address personnel, equipment, and safety issues; facilitated daily conference calls; gathered, recorded, and disseminated event documentation; developed and distributed daily situation reports; provided secure web-based data and information-gathering tools to facilitate situational awareness and operational planning processes; implemented a web-based field reporting and time and mileage websites; and acted as liaison to involved agency administrators and North Carolina Emergency Management.

## OPERATION RESTORE (PEANUT BUTTER RECALL)

In the winter of 2009 the U.S. FDA issued a peanut butter recall due to the recent outbreaks of Salmonella linked to peanut paste. The North Carolina Food and Drug Protection Division conducted 569 checks evaluating over 2,000 products subject to the recall with an effectiveness rate in excess of 68%. The EP Division supported the Food and Drug Division technologically with the creation of a web-based data entry and reporting tools. These tools allowed inspectors in the field to rapidly upload critical time-sensitive data which assisted decision makers, allowing them to make informed choices quickly. Additionally, websites were also developed for workers involved in the recall to record time and mileage, allowing rapid accounting for reimbursement, and an "after-action" website to gather feedback from participants.

## EMERGENCY MANAGEMENT ASSISTANCE COMPACT (EMAC) REQUESTED BY THE ALABAMA DEPARTMENT OF AGRICULTURE AND INDUSTRY TO ASSIST DAMAGED PRODUCER FACILITIES

A poultry depopulation task force consisting of 6 NCDA&CS personnel, resources including 2 foam depopulation units, supplies, and materials deployed to Alabama on May 1, 2011. The focus of this event was response to tornado-damaged poultry producer houses. The task force traveled to Decatur, Alabama and reported to its assigned point of contact. Team A encountered water delivery issues which limited operations to 1 location for the day. This team was operating in concert with a team deployed by others. Two and one-half houses in partial collapse with approximately 24,000 birds were depopulated on this site. Team B was better supplied with water and was able to perform operations on 2 different farms. Two houses in partial collapse on 2 sites with approximately 24,000 birds were depopulated. Operations in both cases resulted in 100% depopulation of houses with no injury to personnel or damage to the equipment.

On day 3 (5/3/2011) the task force was re-assigned to the Alabama Department of Agriculture and Industry. Both teams were directed to a farm on which 4 houses were in total destruction. One pump unit was used to generate foam to depopulate approximately 7,000 birds located in 2 of the houses.

### NCDA&CS EMERGENCY SUPPORT FUNCTION 11 HURRICANE IRENE RESPONSE

Hurricane Irene was a large and powerful Atlantic hurricane that left extensive flood and wind damage along its path through the Caribbean, the U.S. East Coast and as far north as Atlantic Canada in 2011.

In North Carolina, tropical storm force winds began to affect the coastal communities and the Outer Banks hours before landfall, producing waves of 6–9 feet. In addition to the gales, Irene spawned several tornadoes early on August 27 while approaching the coast. Precipitation totals from Irene in the region were particularly high, ranging between 10–14 inches.

Prior to landfall and in anticipation of evacuation in select counties, NCDA&CS EP Division opened the Agriculture Emergency Operations Center and formally established its incident command structure on August 25, 2011, which mirrored the N.C. Emergency Management's activation level. An initial Incident Action Plan was produced and distributed for the operational period beginning at 0700 hrs August 26, 2011 by the NC Agriculture Incident Management Team with the pre-landfall focus of actions centered on public information to protect agricultural infrastructure and farms, the safety of NCDA&CS staff and facilities, operational support of sheltering for animals, and planning of proactive coordination of response actions following landfall.

It's important to note that in April 2011, N.C. Agriculture had another brutal assault by tornadoes that ripped through highly-productive crop land which was just being planted. Agricultural structures and equipment were damaged.

These two events in 2011 resulted in estimated damages of over $450 million to crops and infrastructure; much of which was either not insured at all, or under-insured.

### 2014 NCDA&CS EMERGENCY PROGRAMS DIVISION ACCOMPLISHMENTS

- Internal focus on how to be better prepared as a division to work across lines with sister divisions and across State borders with other agencies to improve capacity in the event of natural or radiological disasters or a food illness outbreak.
- Internally, the division identified an Incident Management Team and invited the Food and Drug Protection Division to join in team training specifically to build capability for managing a large event affecting the food supply.
- North Carolina hosted a training with the USDA APHIS National Veterinary Stockpile team to improve collaboration during disease outbreaks.
- Early in the summer, with news of the West African Ebola Virus (EVD) outbreak and the consequences of managing companion animals of infected individuals coming to North Carolina, EP division began internal discussions while working closely with N.C. Division of Public Health on a strategy for responding to a mission of this type. Through a formal agreement with N.C. Department of Public Health, the EP division is the lead for companion animal care for animals whose owners are exposed to EVD.
- EP division worked collaboratively with the National Alliance for State Animal and Agricultural Emergency Programs (NASAAEP) and the National Animal Rescue and Sheltering Coalition to host their annual meeting and to co-join venues with the 11th Annual One Medicine Symposium.
- EP division staff inspected animal contact exhibits at sanctioned agricultural fairs for compliance with Aedin's Law,[4] while also continuing their educational efforts with fair managers and exhibitors regarding non-contact animal exhibits.

### 2015 NCDA&CS EMERGENCY PROGRAMS DIVISION ACCOMPLISHMENTS

- Chief among the 2015 accomplishments are the multiple deployments of depopulation task forces to Minnesota and Iowa to assist in the depopulation of poultry infected with Highly Pathogenic Avian Influenza (HPAI). Early in the outbreak of HPAI (March, April, and May 2015), both States found themselves

---

[4] After a 2004 outbreak of E. Coli affected 27 people at the North Carolina State Fair, North Carolina legislators passed Aedin's Law, which placed new regulations on petting zoos and animal contact exhibits at agricultural fairs.

in desperate straits as the disease spread rapidly throughout their States; North Carolina's assistance was sought and provided and the State's task forces were able to provide capable assistance to aid in the depopulation of infected poultry/infected premise poultry enabling the spread of the disease to be controlled.

- In offering his thanks to North Carolina, the Minnesota Incident Commander stated with certainty that North Carolina's assistance had "saved the poultry industry in Minnesota."

In reference to North Carolina's second concern, Line Item 18(a) of HSPD–9 speaks to the necessity of developing "A National Veterinary Stockpile (NVS) containing sufficient amounts of animal vaccine, antiviral, or therapeutic products to appropriately respond to the most damaging animal diseases affecting human health and the economy and that will be capable of deployment within 24 hours of an outbreak. The NVS shall leverage where appropriate the mechanisms and infrastructure that have been developed for the management, storage, and distribution of the Strategic National Stockpile."

Foremost in the minds of States in which animal agriculture production is of significant consequence is the possibility of a Foot-and-Mouth Disease (FMD) outbreak. That is certainly the case in North Carolina, home to 9 million hogs.

"Foot and mouth disease is the most important animal disease in the world capable of crossing National boundaries and devastating animal agriculture (a transboundary disease). FMD affects cattle, pigs, sheep, goats, deer, elk, and other wildlife. Ninety-six countries are either endemically or sporadically infected with the disease, therefore there is a constant threat that it will be introduced into the United States either accidentally or intentionally. FMD is extremely contagious and can spread rapidly with devastating consequences. You probably remember the outbreak in the United Kingdom in 2001 which is estimated to have cost approximately $6 billion. The number of livestock and the agriculture economy is much smaller in the United Kingdom than the United States. We learned from their outbreak that we cannot depend on stamping out the disease by killing all infected and exposed animals.

"The size, structure, efficiency, and extensive movement inherent in the United States livestock industry will present unprecedented challenges in the event of an FMD outbreak. No country with a livestock industry comparable to that of the United States has had to deal with an outbreak of FMD, and the impact would extend far beyond animal agriculture.

"Once FMD is detected, an essential tool for control is to stop all animal movement in the affected area. Livestock production in the United States depends on extensive movement of animals. Approximately 400,000 cattle and 1 million swine are estimated to be on the road in trucks each day, either being delivered to packing plants or to other stages of production. Approximately 40 million swine are shipped into a new State each year (~110,000 each day). Many of those cross multiple State lines. In an FMD outbreak, State Animal Health Officials may prohibit animals from an FMD positive area from entering their State. Modern swine production depends on extensive animal movement on a regular basis. If animal movement is stopped, animals will need to be euthanized for welfare reasons because facilities will rapidly become overcrowded.

"An outbreak of FMD will shut down exports of fresh beef, pork, or dairy products. In 2014, beef exports totaled $7.1 billion, pork exports $6.7 billion and dairy exports totaled $7.1 billion. Approximately 11% of U.S. beef production and 22% of U.S. pork production are exported. In 2003, beef exports dropped due to a single case of mad cow disease (BSE); the cumulative loss in U.S. beef trade is estimated to have been $16 billion. The increasing export of beef and pork products in recent years significantly contributes to the value of cattle and swine. As exports increase, the industry becomes more vulnerable to the sudden and extended loss of exports that would result from an FMD outbreak. The price for pork and beef will drop dramatically due to the excess product on the domestic market. That will also impact the price of poultry products and the price of grain.

"In 2011, Dr. Dermot Hayes and colleagues at the Center for Agricultural and Rural Development at Iowa State University published "Economy Wide Impacts of a Foreign Animal Disease in the United States" which had been funded by the National Pork Board. They estimated that over 10 years, the cumulative loss due to an uncontrolled FMD outbreak would be $199.8 billion. Losses estimated include: Pork—$57 billion; Beef—$71 billion; Poultry—$1 billion; Corn—$44 billion; Soybeans—$25 billion; Wheat—$1.8 billion. The impact would likely be larger now because of the increase in the value of exports since 2011. Agriculture is a critical infrastructure in the United States and is severely threatened by the potential of an FMD outbreak.

"The USDA, along with many state and industry officials, recognized that the approach of stamping out and stop movement of animals is simply not possible given the realities of animal agriculture in the United States. The USDA document 'Foot-and-Mouth Disease Vaccination Policy in the United States' (September 2014) illustrates the current capacity of the United States to effectively implement vaccination strategy for control of different types of FMD outbreaks (available upon request). It clearly indicates that there is not sufficient vaccine capacity to assist in controlling an FMD outbreak.

"Fully appreciating the size, structure, efficiency, and extensive movement in the United States livestock industry demonstrates the unprecedented challenges an FMD outbreak would bring about. Control of an FMD outbreak in livestock dense areas without the rapid use of tens of millions of doses of FMD vaccine will be impossible."[5]

That conclusion brings us face-to-face with the dilemma faced by our Nation and our Nation's animal agriculture industry—there are not tens of millions of doses of FMD vaccine available, not anywhere in the world because there is no excess capacity for additional vaccine production—current production capacity meets current day-to-day market needs for FMD vaccine. This same reality was recognized in 2004 when HSPD–9 directed the creation of the National Veterinary Stockpile to respond to the most damaging animal diseases (including FMD) affecting human health and the economy, but NVS has never received sufficient funding to stockpile FMD vaccines.

"It is possible to have an FMD vaccine stockpile available for immediate use. However, establishing and maintaining an FMD vaccine bank is complex. There are 7 distinct serotypes of the virus that are not cross-protective and approximately 65 subtypes. The World Reference Laboratory for FMD recommends that FMD vaccine banks maintain 23 strains of FMD virus in the vaccine bank. Once the virus in the outbreak is isolated, the serotype can be identified and the correct vaccine selected for use.

"A plan to ensure that adequate supplies of FMD vaccine with multiple strains of FMD virus are available in the event of an accidental or intentional introduction of FMD virus into the United States is urgently needed.

"At the request of the National Pork Board, National Cattlemen's Beef Association, and National Milk Producers Federation I produced a white paper entitled 'FMD Vaccine Surge Capacity for Emergency Use in the United States' outlining a potential plan to develop a National Veterinary Stockpile (NVS) with sufficient quantities of FMD vaccine to protect U.S. agriculture, food systems, and the economy. The white paper is available at: *www.cfsph.iastate.edu/pdf/fmd-vaccine-surge-capacity-for-emergency-use-in-the-US.*"[5]

Finally, I will address North Carolina's third concern, the issue of veterinary diagnostic laboratory capacity in North Carolina and across the Nation. Line Item 8 of HSPD–9 states "the Secretaries of the Interior, Agriculture, Health and Human Services, the Administrator of the Environmental Protection Agency, and the heads of other appropriate Federal departments and agencies shall build upon and expand current monitoring and surveillance programs to:

"(c) Develop nation-wide laboratory networks for food, veterinary, plant health, and water quality that integrate existing Federal and State laboratory resources, are interconnected, and utilize standardized diagnostic protocols and procedures."

The National Animal Health Laboratory Network (NAHLN) was developed as a result of this directive and is now part of a Nation-wide strategy to coordinate the work of all organizations providing animal disease surveillance and testing services. NAHLN is an early warning system for emerging and foreign animal diseases and provides surge capacity for the necessary testing during disease outbreaks and during the recovery phase. This surveillance and emergency response system provides critical and on-going resources for laboratory testing, information management, quality assurance and the development and validation of new tests. During the recovery phase testing is necessary to establish a "disease-free status" which also ensures international trading partners of that status.

---

[5] Testimony submitted to the U.S. House of Representatives Agriculture Subcommittee on Livestock and Foreign Agriculture: "Impact of an Outbreak of Foot and Mouth Disease (FMD) in the United States and the Urgent Need for an Adequate Stockpile of FMD Vaccine." Submitted by James A. Roth, DVM, PhD, Director of the Center for Food Security and Public Health, College of Veterinary Medicine, Iowa State University, February 11, 2016.

NAHLN's importance was amply demonstrated during the HPAI outbreaks where thousands of samples were tested within hours in an effort to achieve depopulation of infected flocks within 24 hours. NAHLN performed surveillance in surrounding areas to halt disease spread, to test premises to determine freedom of disease before repopulation could occur, and allow resumption of international trade.

North Carolina's Rollins Veterinary Diagnostic Laboratory, in Raleigh, is one of 12 NAHLN "core laboratories," (so designated because it is one of the original 12 participating laboratories). A Core Member Laboratory receives significant infrastructure support from the U.S. Department of Agriculture (USDA) and conducts fee-for-service testing for USDA. Their funding level enables these laboratories to be fully committed to the NAHLN mission and able to respond to domestic or foreign animal disease emergencies on a 24/7 basis.

NAHLN support comes from USDA–NIFA Food and Agro-Defense Initiative and USDA APHIS. Note: 34 NAHLN labs receive direct State appropriations of $100 million toward total National laboratory operation expenses of $186 million.

As stated at the beginning of the discussion regarding "Efforts to Defend the Nation's Agriculture and Food," I have spoken to 3 HSPD–9 "line items" that are of importance to North Carolina. The first, concerned Line Item 14 of HSPD–9 which directs the participating Departments/agencies to ensure "that the combined Federal, State, and local response capabilities are adequate to respond quickly and effectively . . . ". I trust this testimony allows you to appreciate the wisdom of those in North Carolina who had the foresight to develop the capability that has enabled the State to respond to the myriad events that have transpired over the intervening years—floods, fires, animal disease, human disease, food contamination, drought, and hurricanes, our Emergency Programs Division has been on the forefront of them all—we have been well-served by their efforts. That said, it is also important to note the development of that capability has been funded by the State and through various Federal grants—some $7.3 million in Federal money and $18 million in State money. It is appropriate to note that a remarkable capability, and perhaps a unique capability relative to other States, has been created for a relatively small investment over the years. Consider what similar investments might have meant to states so profoundly affected by HPAI—Iowa and Minnesota experienced as much as $1.6–1.8 billion in economic losses as a result of HPAI on 180 premises. Going forward, continued State and Federal funding will be necessary to maintain current capability, develop new capability, train, exercise, and replace equipment as needed. Unfortunately, funding for North Carolina's Emergency Programs Division continues to decline and places the State's preparedness and response capability at risk.

Of greatest concern for North Carolina is the matter of Line Item 18(a) which speaks to the necessity of developing a National Veterinary Stockpile (NVS) containing sufficient amounts of animal vaccine, antiviral, or therapeutic products to appropriately respond to the most damaging animal diseases—FMD stands alone as North Carolina's greatest threat. The pork industry, the economy, communities, businesses, and families of North Carolina would be devastated by an FMD outbreak; recovery, if a recovery is possible, would be years in the making. A cooperative, collaborative effort, which includes all stakeholders—industry, Federal, State, and academic partners, must be initiated in short order to develop and implement a plan for establishing an effective FMD vaccine stockpile to protect American agriculture.

Lastly, Line Item 8 of HSPD–9 directs the responsible departments and agencies "to develop Nation-wide laboratory networks for food, veterinary, plant health, and water quality that integrate existing Federal and State laboratory resources, are interconnected, and utilize standardized diagnostic protocols and procedures." North Carolina's Veterinary Diagnostic Laboratory System, as a part of the NAHLN, effectively surveilles for and diagnoses animal and zoonotic diseases. However, State and Federal support of and full funding for the Nation's NAHLN laboratory system are necessary to optimize service to stakeholders and the Nation. The absence of full funding was recently noted in the *Bipartisan Report of the Blue Ribbon Study Panel on Biodefense*. The Report states "The National Animal Health Laboratory Network (NAHLN), an effort to detect biological threats to the Nation's food animals, is necessary for effective biosurveillance. The NAHLN is a public-private cooperative effort between the USDA, the American Association of Veterinary Laboratory Diagnosticians, and publicly-funded State veterinary diagnostic laboratories. The collective and integrated work of its members allows for improved detection of emerging and zoonotic diseases, which helps protect animal health, public health, and the food supply. The veterinary diagnostic labs that are members are quite literally on the front lines of disease detection. Established in 2002, the NAHLN is funded through a combination of grants, fee-for-testing services, and administrative support from

USDA. It has struggled to maintain even $10 million worth of annual funding, its appropriations cut over the years to pay for other programs. As a result, the laboratories are unable to meet the threat and have at times eliminated positions and testing capacity for foreign animal diseases. Ten million dollars is a very small price to pay to protect one of America's major industries and portals for disease emergence. After the NAHLN struggled for years to obtain sufficient funding, in 2014 Congress authorized a specific funding line at $15 million per year. NAHLN must be funded to this authorized level in order to meet the need." It is important to note that $5 million was added to NAHLN's budget in 2016 to aid in the response to HPAI; that additional funding was not in the proposed budget for 2017. The request for NAHLN in 2017 remains at $10 million.

Thank you for the opportunity to speak today, on behalf of North Carolina, about issues of concern related to the defense of agriculture and food. I am happy to address any questions you might have.

Ms. McSALLY. Thank you, Dr. Meckes. The Chair now recognizes Dr. Beckham for 5 minutes.

## STATEMENT OF TAMMY R. BECKHAM, D.V.M., PH.D., DEAN, COLLEGE OF VETERINARY MEDICINE, KANSAS STATE UNIVERSITY

Dr. BECKHAM. Good morning, Chairman McSally, Ranking Member Payne, and Members of the House Subcommittee on Emergency Preparedness, Response, and Communication. My name is Tammy Beckham, and I am the dean of the Kansas State College of Veterinary Medicine. Thank you for the opportunity to speak to you today about the role that academia plays in defending our Nation's agriculture and food.

As I testify before you today, U.S. citizens reap the benefits of a robust agricultural industry that provides them with access to a safe, abundant, and affordable food supply. The very elements that make the U.S. agricultural system robust and productive also make it more vulnerable to a natural or intentional introduction of a biological agent. In fact, perhaps now more than ever in any time in our history, our agricultural industries are at risk from a variety of threats that have the potential to severely disrupt our economy, our food supply, and cause great harm to our public health sector.

Threats to our U.S. agricultural sector can come in a variety of forms to include a natural or intentional introduction of a foreign animal emerging and/or a zoonotic disease. Many of the agents that are on the list of those most likely to be utilized execute an agroterror event, such as foot-and-mouth disease, African swine fever or Ebola are readily available in countries throughout the world, and, in particular, in countries in which terrorist groups, such as the Islamic State, al-Qaeda, al-Shabaab, Boko Haram, and others who intend to harm the United States, operate.

Studies indicate the impacts from a natural intentional introduction of any of these agents could lead to devastating economic and public health implications, with the most recent study that was completed by researchers at Kansas State University predicting that the cost associated with foot-and-mouth disease outbreak could result in a total of $188 billion in losses.

Our ability to defend the U.S. livestock industries from these threats is heavily dependent on a coordinated, collaborative, and comprehensive approach involving State and Federal Government, law enforcement industry, both biopharma, and livestock, and academia. Since 2002, with the formation of DHS and the release of

HSPD–9 and HSPD–10, the role of academia and supporting the Homeland Security mission has broadened.

Academia, and, in particular, Land Grant Universities play a very unique and critical role in supporting the agricultural defense mission. Working with our stakeholders and Federal partners, we perform cutting-edge research, we innovate, we develop countermeasures, and solutions, and technologies, that can support our industry during peace time, as well as during a disease outbreak.

Our ability to work in each segment of the development pipeline provides subject-matter expertise, perform research to address specific questions, and act as a hub for reach-back capabilities are just some of the attributes that make academia such a strong and vital partner.

Through our outreach mission, we work diligently to educate producers, stakeholders, and the public about novel technologies, policies, biosecurity practices, and threats to the sector. We have strong relationships with our stakeholders that are built on trust and understanding. Perhaps most importantly, to Homeland Security, provide a venue for a brokered, unbiased discussion and communication between the State and Federal Government and our agriculture sector.

Academia is in a unique position to facilitate discussions between the public and private sector, and oftentimes, works to bridge the communication trust gap so that solutions to complex challenges can be found. Simply stated, we are capable of acting as a trusted partner in what can sometimes be a very complex relationship.

Colleges of veterinary medicine and agriculture across the United States are applying what is arguably their most important role in Homeland Security, and that is teaching, training, and preparing the next generation of Homeland Security workforce. Our graduates do, indeed, understand the role of animal health and success of an agent's agricultural system. Further recognize that veterinarians serve as the first line of defense in identifying incursions of transboundary, emerging, and zoonotic diseases.

I would be remiss not to mention that on a site adjacent to the Kansas State University College of Veterinary Medicine, DHS is currently constructing the National Bio and Agro-Defense facility. Needless to say, close collaboration between NBAF and the KSU CVM and its allied partners presents an inestimal opportunity to further strengthen resources for addressing the threats to the U.S. agriculture and food systems.

There is a need to allocate adequate resources as well to address the Nation's vulnerability in this area. Efforts such as the DHS Centers of Excellence should receive additional resourcing. Additional funds should be provided for agro-defense-focused research through avenues, such as the USDA National Institute for Food and Ag, or NIFA, the National Institutes of Health.

Last, but certainty not least, through increased funding for programs that will be housed within the National bio and agro-defense facility. Indeed, with construction of a state-of-the-art $1.25 billion facility, it is critical to ensure a stable and appropriate level of resources and funding for the research, training, and diagnostic missions that will be housed within it.

Current budgets for the USDA APHIS, ARS, and DHS S&T at Plum Island do not account for the planned expansion of the programs in research, diagnostic, and training that will occur in the new NBAF facility.

So, I urge you today to increase agency programmatic budgets in the future for the NBAF mission so that the full potential of the facility and its DHS and USDA programs and partnerships to include the National Animal Health Laboratory Network can be achieved.

In summary, addressing the threat posed by the intentional or unintentional introduction of a high-consequence disease is a collaborative process. The role of academia in this challenge is but one component of a much broader solution. Preparedness is and will be dependent on a holistic, all-of-enterprise approach in solving this sector's complex problems, and supporting our livestock in allied industries will depend on a strong public-private partnership that is built on trust, collaboration, and resolve.

Finally, Chairman McSally, Ranking Member Payne, and Members of the subcommittee, I want to thank you for the opportunity to speak to you today, and I look forward to your questions.

[The prepared statement of Dr. Beckham follows:]

PREPARED STATEMENT OF TAMMY R. BECKHAM

FEBRUARY 26, 2016

Thank you Chairman Donovan, Ranking Member Payne, and Members of the subcommittee for the honor of addressing you today.

As the dean of the College of Veterinary Medicine at Kansas State University, I am pleased to speak with you regarding "Efforts to Defend the Nation's Agriculture and Food."

U.S. AGRICULTURE: STRENGTHS AND VULNERABILITIES

As first designated in 2003 through Homeland Security Presidential Directive–7, the Food and Agriculture Sector is 1 of 16 critical infrastructures whose assets, systems, and networks are considered to be so vital to the United States that its incapacitation or destruction would have a debilitating effect on security, the National and global economy, public health and safety, or any combination thereof.[1]

The U.S. Agricultural sector is a diverse, complex, and highly-integrated enterprise whose health and productivity is vital to the National economy. Agriculture in the United States is a $1 trillion business and this sector alone employs approximately 9.2% of American workers. In 2013, agriculture and agricultural-related industries contributed $789 billion to the U.S. gross domestic product (GDP), and in 2012 domestic animal agriculture (e.g., livestock and poultry production) produced approximately 1.8 million jobs, $346 billion in total economic output, and $60 billion in household income.[2][3] Furthermore, in the United States, consumers spend on average, approximately 6.4% of their annual expenditures on food. This percentage is extremely low when compared to other countries whose expenditures range from 11% (Switzerland) to 47% (Pakistan).[4] U.S. farmers and ranchers work hard to keep food prices low and are only able to accomplish this through increased efficiencies in production, achieved through technological advancements in industrial food production. Threats that jeopardize our production and the security and affordability

---

[1] Department of Homeland Security. Homeland Security Presidential Directive 7: Critical Infrastructure Identification, Prioritization, and Protection. *http://www.dhs.gov/homeland-security-presidential-directive-7*.

[2] USDA Economic Research Service. *http://ers.usda.gov/data-products/ag-and-food-statistics-charting-the-essentials/ag-and-food-sectors-and-the-economy.aspx*.

[3] Economic benefits of the Livestock Industry. iGrow, South Dakota State University Extension. July 2014.

[4] USDA Economic Research Service. *http://www.ers.usda.gov/data-products/food-expenditures.aspx#.UuE9EHn0Ay5*.

of the U.S. food system have the potential to disrupt our social structure and cause political instability.

The bulk of the agricultural enterprise is almost solely owned and operated by the private sector, and the United States is currently the world's leading exporter of food. When evaluating the impact on the economy, the food supply and the Nation's jobs, it is clearly evident why this industry is deemed a U.S. critical infrastructure. Any disruption to the daily operations and/or productivity of this enterprise would have significant impacts on Americans' livelihoods, our food supply, the economy and our public health. Simply said, U.S. agricultural security is National security.

### THREATS AND VULNERABILITIES OF THE U.S. AGRICULTURAL SYSTEM

As I testify before you today, U.S. citizens reap the benefits of a robust agricultural industry that provides them with access to a safe, abundant, and affordable food supply that is readily available on the shelves of grocery stores Nation-wide. This is indeed a privilege that as you well know, does not exist globally. However, the very elements that make the U.S. agricultural sector robust and productive also make it vulnerable to a natural or intentional introduction of a biological agent. In fact, perhaps now, more than anytime in our history, the agricultural industries are at risk from a variety of threats that have the potential to severely disrupt our economy, our food supply, and cause great harm to our public health sector.

Threats to our U.S. agricultural sector can come in a variety of forms, to include a natural introduction of a foreign (transboundary) animal, emerging, and/or zoonotic disease or an intentional introduction of a biological agent (agroterrorism) into our agricultural systems. These threats would result in significant morbidity and/or mortality among livestock or poultry, cause great economic harm, adversely impact and/or disrupt our food supply, and/or contribute to an adverse public health event. Many of these agents do not require weaponization, can be easily obtained, and exist naturally in areas where terrorist groups such as the Islamic State (ISIS), al-Qaeda, al-Shabaab, Boko Haram, and others who intend to harm the United States operate. In addition, the risk from emerging infectious and/or zoonotic diseases continues to threaten our animal, plant, and public health sectors.

The U.S. agricultural and public health systems, while free from devastating diseases such as Foot and Mouth Disease (FMD, since 1929), African Swine Fever (ASFV), Rift Valley Fever (RVF), and other highly pathogenic livestock and zoonotic diseases, are becoming increasingly at risk for an introduction of these and/or other emerging and/or zoonotic diseases. Impacts resulting from an introduction of a high-consequence disease, agro-terrorist and/or bioterrorist agent into U.S. agricultural systems have been studied and published in peer-reviewed journals. Studies indicate that the magnitude and severity of an introduction of a high-consequence disease into U.S. livestock or poultry herds/flocks would be large. For example, the authors of a study recently completed by Kansas State University predicted that costs associated with an FMD outbreak in the Midwestern United States could result in a total of $188 billion in losses to the livestock and allied industries and up to $11 billion to the U.S. Government.[5]

In addition to publications highlighting the economic and social impacts of a disease incursion, we have learned first-hand from recent experiences that the social, economic, and political fall-out from emerging disease incursions can be devastating. Most recently, the United States has witnessed incursions of porcine epidemic diarrhea virus (PEDV) in our swine populations (2013) and highly pathogenic avian influenza (HPAI) in our poultry populations (2015), as well as Ebola virus (EBOV; 2014) and Zika virus (2016) outbreaks in our public health sector. Each of these events further demonstrates our vulnerability to newly emerging and re-emerging pathogens that can be naturally or intentionally introduced.

In the case of PEDV, the cause and route of introduction into the U.S. swine population has still not clearly been elucidated. Nevertheless, over half of the U.S. sow population was infected with PEDV, and the industry lost 10% (7 million) of the piglets born to these sows during this outbreak.[6] More recently, the introduction of HPAI virus into the U.S. poultry population resulted in the destruction of approximately 7.5 million (7.5%) of the U.S. turkey population and 41.1 million (10%) of the commercial chicken population. The total indemnity cost for this outbreak was

---

[5] Economic impact of alternative FMD emergency vaccination strategies in the Midwestern United States. Ted C. Schroeder, Dustin L. Pendell, Michael W. Sanderson, and Sara McReynolds. Journal of Agricultural and Applied Economics. Volume 47, Issue 01, Feb. 2015. PP 47–78.

[6] PEDv Dominates the Pig World. Gene Johnston. September 11, 2014. *http://www.agriculture.com/livestock/hogs/health/pedv-dominates-pig-wld_284-ar45068*.

approximately $191 million.[7] The PEDV and HPAI outbreaks have reminded us that although we have made significant progress as a Nation and as a sector in preparing for both natural and intentional introductions of transboundary, emerging, and zoonotic diseases, they remain continual threats to the U.S. agricultural system and we still have a tremendous amount of work to accomplish.

The increased risk of the above-mentioned threats to the U.S. agricultural and public health systems can be attributed to several social, environmental, and economic factors. First, there is increased movement of people, animals, plants, and products globally. Global commerce and air traffic moves at speeds that defy the ability to detect and prevent movement of diseases from their source in the early stages before detection. Indeed, animals and people can move and travel prior to clinical signs of a disease, thus arriving in another country already infected and able to spread the disease to people or animals they may contact. Second, trends in livestock production in the United States have resulted in more specialized, intensive, and concentrated farming practices, where large numbers of animals are produced on a much smaller number of premises. These vertically-integrated systems manage movements of animals and animal products to ensure a "just-in-time" delivery to the next location (e.g., feedlot, finisher, packer, and retailer) in the food production system. Our livestock production systems execute a large number of animal movements daily. As an example, it is estimated that approximately 1 million swine and 400,000 cattle are in transit to the next location in the production system at any one time during the day. An introduction of an agent, either naturally or intentionally, into these intensive farming systems could lead to wide-spread distribution through these movements within hours of its introduction. Furthermore, in the event of a disease outbreak in which a "standstill" or quarantine of animal premises is implemented as the primary control strategy, maintaining business continuity through the controlled movements of animals is critical for food security and animal health and welfare.

Next, advanced technical capabilities are not required to obtain agents that can be utilized to promulgate an agro-terrorist event and/or a bioterrorist event against our agriculture and public health systems. Many of the agents on the list of those most likely to be utilized to execute an agro-terrorist and/or bioterrorist event (such as FMDV, ASFV, and Ebola) are readily-available in countries throughout the world and do not need special handling or weaponization. As mentioned previously, these agents are readily available in countries in which terrorist groups such as the Islamic State (ISIS), al-Qaeda, al-Shabaab, Boko Haram, and others who intend to harm the United States operate. Last but certainly not least, we must not overlook the natural occurrence and emergence of diseases whether agricultural or zoonotic. Factors that lead to the emergence of disease include changes in socio-economic, environmental, and/or ecological circumstances.[8] It has been estimated that over 75% of all emerging pathogens are zoonotic and that zoonotic pathogens are twice as likely to be associated with an emerging disease than non-zoonotic pathogens.[9] In addition, there are approximately 320,000 unknown viruses that infect mammals and that have not yet been identified and/or characterized.[10]

Over the last decade, members of the agricultural sector have made tremendous progress in preparing for a natural and/or intentional introduction of a transboundary, emerging and/or high-consequence disease agent. Public and private partnerships have been forged that have paved the way for significant advancements in the development of countermeasures (vaccines, immunomodulators, and diagnostic assays) for high-risk/high-priority agro-terror agents. For example, through a public/private partnership led by the U.S. Department of Homeland Security Science and Technology Directorate (DHS S&T) Agriculture Defense Branch, a conditional U.S. license for the first FMD vaccine that can be manufactured in the United States has been obtained. In addition, we have developed, validated, and deployed (to the National Animal Health Laboratory Network [NAHLN]) molecular assays that are capable of supporting early detection and response for many of the high-risk agroterror agents. And last, but certainly not least, Federal, State, academic, and private partners have worked collaboratively to identify and prioritize risks, scan the global environment, perform comprehensive pathways analysis, and exercise disease

[7] Update on H5Nx, Mia Torchetti, U.S. Department of Agriculture Animal and Plant Health Inspection Service, National Veterinary Services Laobratories, August 18, 2015.

[8] Global trends in emerging infectious diseases. Nature. Kate E. Jones, Nikkita G Patel, Marc A Levy, Adam Storeygard, Deborah Balk, John L Gittleman, Peter Daszak. Volume 451; 21FEB2008.

[9] Taylor, L.H., Latham, S.M., Woolhouse, M.E. 2001. Risk factors for human disease emergence. *Phil Trans R Soc Lond* 356:983–989.

[10] Anthony, S.J., et. al. 2013. A strategy to estimate unknown viral diversity in mammals. MBio 4:e00598–13; doi: 10.1128/mBio.00598–13.

outbreak response plans, all in an effort to enhance resiliency within each component of the sector.

While each of these accomplishments are noteworthy because of their ability to better position our sector to respond to an agro-terror event, they are perhaps more noteworthy because of the breadth of partners that were assembled and worked together collaboratively to accomplish each and every milestone. In the case of the FMD vaccine, DHS S&T, U.S. Department of Agriculture Animal and Plant Health Inspection Service (USDA APHIS) and Agricultural Research Service (USDA ARS), biopharma, the livestock industries, and academia were all essential players in ensuring development, transition, and ultimate licensure of this product. Indeed, many more of these unique partnerships are needed and are, in fact, critical to ensuring our success. We have enjoyed many successes, but still have much to accomplish if we are to be fully prepared when, not if, a devastating natural or intentional introduction of one of these agents occurs.

PUBLIC AND PRIVATE-SECTOR PREVENTION, PLANNING & PREPAREDNESS ACTIVITIES: THE ACADEMIC ROLE

Our ability to defend U.S. Agriculture and Food from the threat of intentional, unintentional, or inadvertent introduction of high-consequence disease is heavily dependent on a coordinated, collaborative, and comprehensive approach involving both State and Federal government, law enforcement, industry (biopharma and animal producers), and academia. We must work together as members of the agricultural enterprise to leverage expertise, develop technologies and networks and/or systems that will ultimately produce a more resilient agriculture and food system.

Building on my previous roles with the Federal Government and academia, and in my current role as the dean of the KSU College of Veterinary Medicine, I take the security of our livestock and poultry systems very seriously, and respect the role of academia in this broader partnership. Furthermore, I know that preparedness stems from true partnerships and collaborations across the enterprise and it is only through leveraging expertise throughout all levels of the sector that we will meet the challenge of securing our Nation's agriculture and food supply.

Since the formation of DHS in 2002, and with the release of Homeland Security Presidential Directive 9: Defense of United States Agriculture and Food (HSPD–9), DHS has assumed the responsibility to coordinate the overall National effort to protect the critical infrastructure and key resources of the United States, which includes agriculture. However, the USDA still has the primary responsibility for protecting the agricultural sector [11] and does so with support from additional agencies to include the Department of Health and Human Services (DHHS), the Department of Interior (DOI), the Environmental Protection Agency (EPA), the Federal Bureau of Investigation (FBI), the Central Intelligence Agency (CIA), the Department of Defense (DOD), and the Attorney General (AG).

Academia, and in particular the Land Grant Universities, play a very unique and critical role in supporting the agricultural defense mission. Working with our stakeholders and Federal partners (USDA, DHS, and other State and Federal agencies), we perform cutting-edge and innovative research to develop countermeasures (e.g., vaccines, diagnostics, and immunomodulators), solutions, and technologies that can support our industry during peacetime, as well as in the event of a high-consequence disease and/or agro-terror event. Furthermore, through our teaching and outreach missions, we work diligently to train the next generation workforce and educate producers, stakeholders, and the public about novel technologies, policies, biosecurity practices, animal welfare, threats to the agricultural sector and much more. It is through these activities that our faculty and staff have developed strong relationships with producers, stakeholders, livestock owners, the allied industries and other National associations (e.g., National Pork Board, National Cattlemen's Beef Association). These relationships are built on trust and understanding and perhaps most importantly to homeland security and protection of the agricultural sector, provide a venue for a brokered, unbiased discussion and communication between the State and Federal Government and our agricultural sector. Academia is in a unique position to facilitate discussion between the public and private sector and oftentimes works to bridge the communication and trust gap so that solutions to complex challenges can be found. Simply stated, we are capable of acting as a "trusted partner" in what can sometimes be a complex relationship.

Since 2002, with the formation of DHS and the release of HSPD–9 (Defense of the United States Agriculture and Food) and HSPD–10 (Biodefense for the 21st

---

[11] Public Health Security and Bioterrorism Preparedness Response Act, 2002. *http:// www.gpo.gov/fdsys/pkg/PLAW-107publ188/pdf/PLAW-107publ188.pdf.*

Century), the role of academia in supporting the homeland security mission and, more specifically in protecting our agriculture and food sector from an agro-terror threat, has broadened. HSPD–9 not only called for DHS to accelerate and expand development of current and new countermeasures against the intentional introduction or natural occurrence of catastrophic animal, plant and zoonotic diseases, it also called for the Secretaries of Homeland Security and Agriculture to establish university-based Centers of Excellence (COEs) in agriculture and food security. As a result of this directive, there are two COEs within the DHS S&T Office of University Programs (OUP) that are focused on agriculture and food security: The Zoonotic and Animal Disease Defense (ZADD), co-led by Kansas State University and Texas A&M University, and the Food Protection and Defense Institute (FPDI), formerly the National Center for Food Protection and Defense (NCFPD), led by the University of Minnesota. The primary mission of each of these Centers is to work across the agricultural enterprise to create novel solutions to homeland security challenges. Each of these Centers works closely with State and Federal partners, as well as the industries to ensure portfolio alignment with Nationally-identified priorities. Each COE has a robust set of partner universities, National and international collaborators and stakeholders that are routinely brought together in multi-institutional, multi-disciplinary teams to address the complex challenges that face our industries today.

In light of the aforementioned roles and responsibilities, and in the context of a broadening academic presence in supporting homeland security, I would like to highlight a few instances in which academia has worked with other members of the agricultural enterprise to deliver products and/or technologies that have strengthened our Nation's ability to respond to and recover from a potential agro-terror event. In addition, I would like to touch on several on-going activities, each with a strong academic role, that demonstrate the power of partnerships and strength of a holistic approach to combatting a potential terror event.

Over the past decade, the University COEs have worked closely with DHS S&T, USDA (APHIS and ARS), State Animal Health Officials (SAHOs), biopharma, and our livestock industries to identify and address National gaps in agriculture and food security. In particular DHS has sponsored multiple COE-led workshops that have convened producers, livestock owners, National organizations, State and Federal agencies, as well as industry and academia to identify and prioritize gaps, provide recommendations for addressing those gaps and help set National priorities for policy development and funding. For example, the agricultural screening tools workshops, designed to identify gaps in screening tools and diagnostics for high consequence agro-terror agents, helped develop and guide a robust program in diagnostic assay development. As a result of this program, multiple assays for early detection and/or recovery were developed, validated, and either accepted by the NAHLN for use during an animal disease event (FMD bulk tank milk assay), or transitioned to an industry partner for production and licensure (3B FMD ELISA). It was through intensive planning and partnership that each of the steps in development of these assays was accomplished. Academia, and in particular the COEs worked with DHS, USDA APHIS, and ARS, the livestock industry and biopharma to lead the development and transition of each assay, working diligently to ensure the assays met each of their requirements.

The role that academia plays in the development, piloting, and transitioning of veterinary countermeasures and/or technologies cannot be overstated. Our ability to work in each segment of the development pipeline makes us unique in our capability to support the homeland security enterprise. During the last 6 years, the ZADD Center has enjoyed tremendous success in working with our Federal and State partners, biopharma, and the livestock industries to develop, transition, pilot, and ultimately license multiple products to aid in the detection or response to an agro-terror event. For example, the Center of Excellence in Emerging and Zoonotic Animal Diseases (CEEZAD), which is housed within the CVM at Kansas State University, is currently working with an animal health company to develop, test, and evaluate a novel recombinant vaccine for Rift Valley Fever virus (RVFV), a high-consequence transboundary/zoonotic disease agent. If successful, this product will be produced, licensed, and available for purchase by the USDA APHIS National Veterinary Stockpile, should the need arise. CEEZAD's unique relationships with the biopharmaceutical industry allows for early input and buy-in regarding the products being developed within the Center. This increases the likelihood of acceptance, production, and eventual licensure of DHS S&T OUP sponsored research.

In addition, the DHS S&T Agriculture Defense Branch has engaged the COE at Texas A&M University, the Institute for Infectious Animal Diseases (IIAD), and tasked them with working to develop a template, obtain permits, and forge relationships that will allow for the first-ever international field trial of the newly-licensed

FMD vaccine. If successful, this template will provide a robust guideline for performing a successful field trial, but more than that, it will provide a template, standard operating procedures, and solidify relationships that will be critical for supporting additional testing of future DHS S&T products in an international field-trial setting. Both of the aforementioned projects are excellent examples of how the DHS S&T Chemical and Biological Division (CBD) and DHS S&T OUP are working with a broad spectrum of partners, both individually and through academia, to enhance our Nation's agriculture and food security.

Next, the USDA APHIS has worked closely with the Center for Food Security and Public Health (CFSPH) at Iowa State University to develop the Secure Food Supply Plans (eggs, turkeys, milk, pork, and beef). In the event of an animal disease outbreak, our industries must be able to resume movements from disease-free premises within a short amount of time. Any delay in this ability will result not only in product shortages but also in serious animal welfare issues. Supported by the USDA APHIS and led by an academic partner (CFSPH), the livestock and poultry industry, allied industries, State and Federal partners, and other stakeholders worked cooperatively to develop and vet each individual sector-specific plan. This multi-partner effort has resulted in the development of robust templates and guidance documents that can be utilized by State animal health officials for permitting movements of animals and animal products from disease-free premises in the event of an animal disease emergency.

In addition to the examples given above, DHS S&T, SAHOs and the USDA engage academia for expertise in epidemiology, modeling, surveillance, pathology, immunology, and many other fields. Our ability to provide subject-matter expertise, perform research to address specific questions, and act as a hub for reach-back capabilities are just some of the attributes that make us a strong and vital partner.

Last but certainly not least, Colleges of Veterinary Medicine and Agriculture across the United States are playing what is arguably their most important role in homeland security, and that is: Teaching, training, and preparing the next-generation homeland security workforce.

The State of Kansas has a proud history of agricultural production, and it continues to be among the leading States in the Nation for crop and animal industry. For example, in 2014, Kansas ranked first among the States for production of sorghum for grain (200 million bushels), second for wheat (250 million bushels), third for commercial red meat production (5 billion pounds), and third in production of cattle and calves (6 million head).[12] At K-State's College of Veterinary Medicine, we instill a respect for this agricultural enterprise and its relevance in feeding our Nation and the world among our students. The KSU CVM is one of the oldest veterinary colleges in the United States, and has graduated more than 5,000 men and women veterinarians. As opposed to many other veterinary schools, where the majority of students pursue small animal medicine, KSU prides itself on a strong focus on production animal medicine, which is put into practice by our Department of Clinical Sciences. Indeed, these graduates understand the role of animal health in the success of the Nation's agricultural system, and further recognize that veterinarians serve as the first line of defense in identifying incursions of transboundary, emerging, and zoonotic diseases.

In the interest of developing the next generation of animal health professionals, the KSU CVM maintains a number of educational programs, including those in veterinary medicine, advanced clinical training, and research in animal health and related disciplines. The CVM's Department of Diagnostic Medicine/Pathobiology encompasses a number of research program thrusts that are directly relevant to defense of U.S. Agriculture. For example, a number of programs are focused on all aspects of infectious disease and include viral and bacterial pathogenesis of endemic and emerging diseases, vaccine and antiviral development and evaluation, diagnostic assay development and validation, epidemiology and ecology of infectious disease, and the study of vector-borne diseases. Researchers within the CVM also work closely with the KSU Biosecurity Research Institute (BRI), a biocontainment research and education facility. The BRI supports comprehensive "farm-to-fork" infectious disease research programs that address threats to plant, animal, and human health. The BRI facilitates diverse and multidisciplinary research and training opportunities, with the capability for research on foreign animal diseases in both large and small animal models, and basic and applied research. Faculty at the KSU CVM are working collaboratively with the BRI on projects addressing many of the highest-threat disease agents (e.g., Classical Swine Fever, African Swine Fever, and Rift Valley Fever).

---

[12] Kansas Department of Agriculture. Kansas Farm Facts. *http://agriculture.ks.gov/docs/default-source/Kansas-Farm-Facts-2015/kansasfarmfacts2014final.pdf?sfvrsn=4.*

On a site adjacent to the KSU CVM and BRI, DHS is currently constructing the National Bio and Agro-Defense Facility (NBAF). This facility will serve to replace and augment the mission currently being performed by the Plum Island Animal Disease Center. The NBAF will "be a state-of-the-art biocontainment laboratory for the study of diseases that threaten both America's animal agricultural industry and public health . . . [offering capabilities] to conduct research, develop vaccines, diagnose emerging diseases, and train veterinarians."[13] Needless to say, close collaboration between the NBAF and the KSU CVM and its allied partner programs, presents inestimable opportunities to further strengthen local and regional resources for addressing threats to U.S. Agriculture and Food.

CONCLUSION AND RECOMMENDATIONS

As I've described, addressing the threat posed by the intentional or unintentional introduction of a high-consequence disease is a collaborative process. The role of academia is only part of a much broader solution. Across the Federal Government, programs in agencies such as Health and Human Services (HHS), the Department of Defense, U.S. Agency for International Development, U.S. Geological Survey, and the Environmental Protection Agency must come together with USDA (APHIS and ARS) and DHS. Similarly, engagement of industry stakeholders from dairy, pork, beef, and poultry, as well as the allied industries, must occur to ensure that technological solutions and operational response measures are viable. Given the availability of high-consequence infectious agents abroad, a holistic approach to bio- and agro-defense must also involve threat reduction at the global level. This should involve multi-national collaborators such as the Defense Threat Reduction Agency (DTRA), the Food and Agriculture Organization of the United Nations (UN FAO) and the World Organization for Animal Health (OIE) to name a few.

In addition to the need for collaboration there is also a need to allocate adequate resources to address the Nation's vulnerability in this area. Considering the significance of agriculture to the American public's well-being, measures should be taken to correct the drastic imbalance in research and countermeasure funding for agriculturally-focused threats, versus human-centric ones. For example, during fiscal year 2014, 61% of Federal funding for biodefense was allocated to HHS, while USDA received only 1%.[14] Similarly, the Strategic National Stockpile, which houses the Nation's repository of antibiotics, vaccines, chemical antidotes, antitoxins, and other critical medical equipment and supplies, received approximately $510 million, while the National Veterinary Stockpile received approximately $4 million. As further evidence of this imbalance, in 2007, the Laboratory Response Network, an integrated network of State and local public health, Federal, military, and international laboratories that can respond to bioterrorism, chemical terrorism and other public health emergencies, had an annual budget of approximately $50 million[15] while the NAHLN receives only $6 million dollars annually to support its operations.

There is also a need to increase emphasis on educational programs to further support U.S. Agriculture and Food. Efforts such as the DHS Centers of Excellence should receive additional resourcing, and U.S. veterinary curricula should emphasize the changing role of the veterinarian as part of a global defense against high-consequence transboundary, emerging, and/or zoonotic diseases. Additional funds should be provided for agro-defense-focused research, through avenues such as the USDA National Institute of Food and Agriculture (NIFA), the National Institutes of Health (NIH) and lastly but not least, through increased funding for programs that will be housed within the National Bio and Agro-Defense Facility (NBAF). Indeed, with construction of a state-of-the-art $1.25 billion facility, it is critical to ensure a stable and appropriate level of resources and funding for the research, training and diagnostic missions that will be housed within it. Currently, budgets for the USDA APHIS, ARS, and DHS S&T at PIADC do not account for the planned expansion of research/diagnostic/training programs that will occur in the new NBAF facility. I urge you to increase agency programmatic budgets for the NBAF mission, so that the full potential of the facility, and its DHS and USDA programs, can be achieved.

Preparedness for a natural or intentional introduction of a high-consequence agricultural event is dependent on a holistic, all-of-enterprise approach. Solving this sec-

---

[13] Department of Homeland Security. National Bio and Agro-Defense Facility. *http://www.dhs.gov/science-and-technology/national-bio-and-agro-defense-facility.*

[14] Sell, T.K. and Watson, M. Federal Agency Biodefense Funding, FY2013–FY2014. Biosecurity and Bioterrorism: Biodefense Strategy, Practice, and Science. Volume 11, Number 2, 2013. PP 196–216.

[15] State Public Health Laboratories: Sustaining Preparedness in an Unstable Environment. March 2009, Association of Public Health Laboratories.

tor's complex problems and supporting our industries will depend on a strong public/private partnership that is built on trust, collaboration, and resolve.

Finally, Chairman Donovan, Ranking Member Payne, and Members of the subcommittee, I want to thank you for this opportunity to speak to you regarding efforts to defend the Nation's agriculture and food. I look forward to your questions.

Ms. McSALLY. Thank you. The Chair recognizes Mr. Acord for 5 minutes.

### STATEMENT OF BOBBY ACORD, FORMER ADMINISTRATOR, ANIMAL PLANT HEALTH INSPECTION SERVICE, U.S. DEPARTMENT OF AGRICULTURE, TESTIFYING ON BEHALF OF THE NATIONAL PORK PRODUCERS COUNCIL

Mr. ACORD. Madam Chairwoman, Ranking Member Payne, Members of the subcommittee, the U.S. Department of Agriculture industry and the U.S. food supply always have been at great risk from pest and disease. That risk has continued to increase over the years because of increases in travel, tourism, and trade, each passenger handbag, each piece of luggage brought into the United States poses a risk. Every parcel mailed to the United States poses a risk. Large volumes of commodities and products from a wide range of countries are transported legally, and some illegally, to the United States every year by different conveyances, all of which may be carrying a disease or hitchhiking pest.

Now the country faces a new risk: Terrorists weaponizing disease to inflict harm on the U.S. economy. Of particular concerns of the livestock industry is foot-and-mouth disease. It is a highly contagious viral disease affecting all cloven-hoofed animals. The structure of the U.S. livestock industry makes the United States particularly vulnerable to a large-scale foot-and-mouth disease outbreak. There are an estimated 1 million pigs and 400,000 cattle moved daily in the United States, some over long distances. There are numerous auctions, fairs, exhibits that concentrate large numbers of animals in a single location. Those movements and concentrations provide opportunities for just one infected or exposed animal to infect many others.

The U.S. industry is also concerned about African swine fever that has reared its ugly head in Russia, Belarus, and eastern European countries that border Russia and those other countries. It is a disease for which there is no means of control. As Dr. Meckes mentioned, there is an insufficient quantity of foot-and-mouth vaccine. With support of the livestock industry, APHIS changed its policy on managing a foot-and-mouth disease outbreak from culling all infected and exposed animals to one of vaccination in all but the smallest of outbreaks.

When discussing how this policy would be implemented, it became apparent that there is not enough vaccine to deal with an outbreak, and there is no capability of producing a sufficient quantity to deal with an outbreak in the United States.

The livestock industry has made it clear that a solution to the vaccine shortage must include a contract for an offshore vendor-maintained bank that includes antigen for all 23 FMD types that are currently circulating in the world, and that a contract be awarded for surge capacity to produce sufficient quantities of vaccine in the event of an outbreak in the livestock herd.

There are gaps in the U.S. biosecurity system. Most outbreaks, the first problem encountered is the lack of biosecurity, which contributes to the spread of the disease. One solution to this problem is that in addition to test exercises, the Federal and State agencies need a more robust review of biosecurity measures in each section of the agriculture industry.

We need more robust scrutiny of imports. Federal agencies are relying too much on the ports of entry as the first line of defense against pest disease introduction. More emphasis must be placed on what happens during processing production of products in the countries of origin.

We had an outbreak of Porcine Epidemic Diarrhea in the United States in 2013, and the means and the method by which that introduction was brought to the United States has never been discovered. If that gap in the security system is still open, then it is open for FMD and all other diseases as well.

We have a serious problem with animal traceability in this country. It is inadequate for the use in an animal disease outbreak. In fact, it is not even recognized as adequate to meet the requirements of some of the major U.S. trading partners. Many of the shortfalls identified today are the result of lack of adequate resources, risks to U.S. agriculture and the U.S. food supply have increased dramatically over the last few years, and have now been exacerbated by the threat of terrorist targeting agriculture production. At the same time, funding provided to maintain the country's safeguarding system has been reduced. We simply can't have it both ways.

In conclusion, there seems to be a growing consensus that there are serious flaws in the country's preparedness to deal with threats to the U.S. agriculture and the food supply. The bipartisan report of the Blue Ribbon Study Panel on Biodefense highlighted the need for improvements in the system for protecting U.S. livestock herd in the Nation's food supply.

A lot of information has been gathered from that report, from the hearings that you have held, from hearings that have been held at the Department of Agriculture—excuse me, by the Committee on Agriculture. There is a lot of information that has now been developed, and it seems that from the perspective of the National Pork Producers Council and probably, more largely, the livestock industry, it is now time to catch and to work with the Obama administration to let's fill these gaps, and let's not continue to just look, let's act at this point. Thank you, and I would be happy to answer any questions.

[The prepared statement of Mr. Acord follows:]

PREPARED STATEMENT OF BOBBY ACORD

FEBRUARY 26, 2016

INTRODUCTION

The National Pork Producers Council (NPPC) is an association of 43 State pork producer organizations that serves as the global voice in Washington, DC, for the Nation's pork producers. The U.S. pork industry represents a significant value-added activity in the agricultural economy and the overall U.S. economy. Nationwide, more than 68,000 pork producers marketed more than 110 million hogs in 2014, and those animals provided total gross receipts of $23.4 billion. Overall, an estimated $22.3 billion of personal income and $39 billion of Gross National Product are supported by the U.S. pork industry.

Economists Daniel Otto, Lee Schulz, and Mark Imerman at Iowa State University estimate that the U.S. pork industry is directly responsible for the creation of more than 37,000 full-time equivalent pork-producing jobs and generates about 128,000 jobs in the rest of agriculture. It is responsible for approximately 102,000 jobs in the manufacturing sector, mostly in the packing industry, and 65,000 jobs in professional services such as veterinarians, real estate agents, and bankers. All told, the U.S. pork industry is responsible for nearly 550,000 mostly rural jobs in the United States, and U.S. pork producers today provide 23 billion pounds of safe, wholesome, and nutritious meat protein to consumers world-wide.

## DISEASE AND PEST INTRODUCTIONS

The U.S. agriculture industry and the U.S. food supply always have been at great risk from pests and disease. That risk has continued to increase over the years because of increases in travel, tourism, and trade. Each passenger handbag and piece of luggage brought into the United States and every parcel mailed to this country presents a risk of transporting disease to some sector of the agriculture industry. Large volumes of commodities and products from a wide range of countries are transported legally and illegally to the United States each year by different conveyances, all of which may be carrying a disease or hitchhiking pest. Now the country faces a new risk: Terrorists weaponizing disease as a means of inflicting harm on the U.S. economy. Whether by accident or deliberate introduction, the impact of a disease or pest on U.S. agriculture and the food supply could be devastating.

Over the last few years, the United States has seen numerous introductions of pests and diseases that have affected agriculture production. Citrus Canker and Citrus Greening are wrecking havoc on the Florida citrus industry. Other pests that serve as disease vectors have had a serious impact on fruit and vegetable production in other parts of the country, particularly California. In April 2013, Porcine Epidemic Diarrhea infected a swine herd in Ohio, and it spread rapidly through most of the U.S. swine industry, resulting in an estimated loss of more than 8 million newborn pigs, which took an emotional toll on producers and ultimately increased prices to consumers. Subsequently 2 other swine diseases of Asian origin were discovered, Delta Corona Virus and Orthoreovirus. In 2015, High Pathogenic Avian Influenza (HPAI) was discovered in poultry flocks in the Midwest, resulting in the culling of millions of turkeys and laying hens, particularly in Iowa and Minnesota.

## CURRENT THREATS

When compared with many countries in the world, U.S. agriculture is relatively free of pests and disease. Through cooperation between the Government and agriculture industries, some of the most serious pests and diseases have been eradicated. Foot and Mouth Disease (FMD), Classical Swine Fever (CSF), Pseudorabies in swine, Screwworm, Cotton Boll Weevil, and numerous fruit fly infestations have all been successfully eradicated but at great cost to taxpayers and the affected industries. Yet all these diseases and pests still lurk around the world, some very close to the U.S. mainland, and are still serious threats.

Of particular concern to the livestock industry is FMD, a highly contagious viral disease affecting all cloven-hoofed animals. FMD is easily spread by livestock movement, wind currents, on vehicles that have traveled to and from infected farms and on inanimate objects that have come in contact with the virus. This economically devastating disease is endemic in 113 countries around the world. In 2014, the World Organization for Animal Health (OIE) reported 779 FMD outbreaks in member countries. The structure of the U.S. livestock industry makes the United States particularly vulnerable to a large-scale FMD outbreak. There are an estimated 1 million pigs and 400,000 cattle moved daily in the United States, some over long distances, and there are numerous auctions, fairs, and exhibits that concentrate large numbers of animals in a single location. Those movements and concentrations provide opportunities for 1 infected or exposed animal to spread disease to a large number of animals and over long distances.

The U.S. swine industry also is very concerned about the emergence of African Swine Fever (ASF) in Russia, the Ukraine, Belarus, and the Eastern European countries of Estonia, Latvia, Lithuania, and Poland. ASF is a highly contagious viral disease for which there is no vaccine or method of control except strict biosecurity and culling of infected animals. The disease has become endemic in those countries' feral swine populations, with occasional spread to backyard pigs and commercial production. An ASF introduction in the United States would be devastating to the U.S. pork industry.

Also of great concern is CSF. Previously eradicated from the United States, it lurks very close to the U.S. mainland in Hispaniola. It is also prevalent in Central and South America and other countries around the world. Vaccines are available and stockpiled for use, but an outbreak in the United States would have serious economic consequences.

While the above highlighted diseases are the livestock industry's worst fears, the U.S. Department of Agriculture's Animal and Plant Health Inspection Service (APHIS) focuses on preventing 160 animal diseases from entering the United States. Animal and plant diseases can be devastating to agriculture production, but the high value of animal agriculture makes introduction of animal diseases far more economically significant. Pests and diseases of concern are monitored by U.S. authorities through port-of-entry inspections and surveillance by APHIS and State departments of agriculture.

### CONSEQUENCES OF PEST AND DISEASE INTRODUCTION

Introduction of pests and diseases can have severe economic consequences for agriculture production, consumer prices and, potentially, food availability. Also of great concern is the loss of export markets. The United States is required by the International Plant Protection Convention (IPPC) and the OIE to report pest and disease introductions that are listed by those international bodies as economically significant or trade limiting or that are new or emerging diseases. In most cases, such reporting would result in an immediate loss of exports for the affected commodity or products, causing a precipitous drop in U.S. market prices.

The economic consequences of disease introduction are often not limited to just one agriculture sector. Iowa State University economist Dermot Hayes estimates that an FMD outbreak in the United States would result in revenue losses to the beef and pork industries of $12.9 billion per year over a 10-year period; the corn and soybean industries are estimated to lose $44 billion and $24.9 billion, respectively. These estimates do not include losses to the dairy industry. Also, they do not include the costs, which are likely to be millions of dollars, to the Federal and State governments for culling, vaccinating, and other activities associated with controlling the disease.

### IMPROVED PROTECTION

There have been several improvements in the systems to safeguard U.S. agriculture. Creating the Bureau of Customs and Border Protection (BCBP) and combining APHIS's agriculture inspectors into that single agency has been a positive development. In the early stages of the reorganization, there appeared to be a lack of focus by BCBP on the importance of agriculture inspections, but pressure from the agriculture industries and Members of Congress resulted in significant improvements over time. Anecdotal evidence gathered through interviews with agriculture inspectors formerly housed in APHIS suggests improved enforcement of agriculture regulations through use of the broader enforcement authority of BCBP. However, much remains to be done to improve the ability of the United States to exclude plant and animal pests and diseases from entering the country.

APHIS has worked with the animal agriculture industries to develop Secure Food Supply Plans for pork, beef, milk, turkeys, and eggs. The plans, which are in various stages of development, focus on tightened biosecurity and compartmentalization of diseases to allow movement of animals to slaughter and products to the marketplace. They also allow for movement of live animals within a compartment. If the United States can gain acceptance of these plans by its trading partners, it will lessen the economic impact of a disease.

Communications among State and Federal agencies also have improved, and the Department of Homeland Security has assisted with exercises to test the country's preparedness for disease outbreaks. Additionally, creation of the Food and Agriculture Sector Coordinating Council has raised awareness of the need for biosecurity throughout the food chain.

### VULNERABILITIES

Even though there have been significant improvements in the systems for safeguarding U.S. agriculture and the Nation's food supply, there are still significant vulnerabilities and challenges that must be addressed. They include:

*An insufficient quantity of FMD vaccine.*—With support of the livestock industry, APHIS changed its policy on managing an FMD outbreak from culling all infected and exposed animals to one of vaccination in all but the smallest of outbreaks. Based on experience with outbreaks in the United Kingdom and Korea, the United States simply cannot euthanize its way out of an outbreak; vaccination is the only realistic alternative. When discussing how this policy would be implemented, it became apparent that to deal with an outbreak there was not enough vaccine available nor could a sufficient quantity be obtained in time to implement an effective control program.

The United States is the only country in the world that maintains its own vaccine antigen bank, and it serves all of North America. The bank is maintained at the Plum Island Animal Disease Center (PIADC) on Plum Island, NY, and has a limited number of antigens. Under the current manufacturer(s)' contract, antigen is shipped to Europe where it is made into finished vaccine that then is shipped back to the United States. After 3 weeks, this process would produce only 2.5 million doses of vaccine. Dr. James Roth, professor and researcher at Iowa State University, estimates that at least 10 million doses would be needed during the first 2 weeks of an outbreak. Currently, there is no surge capacity to produce additional doses of vaccine. All the vaccine production capacity in the world is currently in use by other countries.

Current law prohibits live FMD virus from being introduced onto the U.S. mainland, so foreign production companies are the only source of finished vaccine. It has been suggested that recombinant DNA vaccines that do not use live FMD virus can be produced in the United States, thus avoiding the legal prohibition of having live virus on the mainland. However, current data is not sufficient to determine how quickly, and indeed whether, such vaccines provide protection outside the laboratory environment and for all species. The United States is likely years away from the development and commercialization of such novel vaccines. While developing such a vaccine would be a positive move, the reality is that the U.S. livestock industry must have vaccines that are protective against the strain of FMD that might be in a sample sitting at the PIADC for analysis at this very moment!

The House Agriculture Committee's Subcommittee on Livestock and Foreign Agriculture held a hearing Feb. 11, 2015, on the FMD vaccine shortage. The livestock industry made it clear that a solution to the vaccine shortage must include a contract for an offshore, vendor-maintained bank that includes antigen for all 23 FMD types that are currently circulating in the world and that a contract be awarded for surge capacity to produce sufficient quantities of vaccine for an outbreak in the U.S. livestock herd.

*Gaps in U.S. biosecurity.*—Both USDA and DHS focus a lot of attention on test exercises, and those are very beneficial activities. In most outbreaks, the first problem encountered is the lack of biosecurity, which contributes to the spread of disease. By the time adequate biosecurity is established the disease has been spread over much larger areas and control becomes much more challenging and costly. Test exercises do not accurately reveal what happens during an actual outbreak.

Current pork production methods concentrate large numbers of animals in a single location, and the pork industry has always prided itself on having a robust biosecurity system. However, during the PEDv outbreak in 2013, the industry discovered serious gaps in biosecurity that contributed to spreading the disease. The same problem was also identified in the HPAI outbreak in 2015.

One solution to this problem is that, in addition to test exercises, Federal and State agencies need a more robust review of biosecurity measures in each sector of the agriculture industry. Producers and their allied industries should be provided resources to increase training on the importance of biosecurity and how to identify gaps in their systems. While this would require additional resources, the potential savings to the Government are significant, providing a very favorable cost/benefit ratio.

*More robust scrutiny of imports.*—Federal agencies are relying too much on the ports of entry as the first line of defense against pest and disease introduction. More emphasis must be placed on what happens during processing and production of products in the countries of origin. With most cargo being moved in containers, thorough inspection at the port of entry is virtually impossible. APHIS prepares risk assessments for all plant- and animal-origin products moving into U.S. territory, and in many cases those assessments are based on information supplied by Government officials and do not always include a site visit. Further, because of resource constraints, there is not enough follow up to assure that risk mitigations are being followed.

The U.S. Food and Drug Administration is responsible for inspection of feed and feed ingredients produced in foreign countries and in the United States. Not enough resources are being made available to APHIS and FDA to do a thorough inspection of foreign manufacturers to determine if they are following good manufacturing practices and if Government regulation and oversight are effective. That shortfall increases the risk to U.S. agriculture of disease introduction.

The strain of the PED virus introduced into the United States was determined to be of Chinese origin. But Government officials responsible for overseeing port-of-entry inspections and disease risk management have been unable to specifically identify the source or means of introduction of the virus even though APHIS conducted a root cause investigation. If there were a gap in the U.S. safety net that allowed the recent introduction of PEDv and Delta Corona virus, it also remains open for FMD!

*Traceability.*—The U.S. pork industry has been a vocal advocate for a robust Nationally-standardized mandatory system for animal traceability. APHIS spent years working on a system of individual animal identification to allow accurate tracing of the movement of livestock, which is an absolutely critical component of any system for managing disease. Unfortunately, opposition from some sectors of the livestock community resulted in a compromise that provided only a State-based system that requires each State to be able to trace livestock movements within its State. The current traceability system is inadequate for use in a disease outbreak. In fact, it is not even recognized as adequate to meet the requirements of some major U.S. trading partners.

*Resource constraints.*—Many of the shortfalls identified in this testimony result from of a lack of adequate resources. Risks to U.S. agriculture and the U.S. food supply have increased dramatically over the last few years and have now been exacerbated by the threat of terrorists targeting agriculture production. At the same time, funding provided to maintain the country's safeguarding systems have been reduced. It is hard to conceive that enough efficiencies can be found to address an increasing threat and save money at the same time. Collectively, the agriculture industry, the Obama administration and Congress must face the reality that addressing these serious shortcomings in the U.S. safety net will require a significant outlay of additional funds. We can't have it both ways! The history of Government involvement in disasters such as disease outbreaks is that once an outbreak occurs unlimited resources are committed to getting control of the situation. The savings everyone wants to make can be achieved by investing now in the Nation's preparedness and avoiding a more costly disease eradication program in the future.

*Gaps in early detection.*—Early disease detection and rapid response to any outbreak provide the best opportunity to limit the spread of Foreign Animal Diseases (FADs). Even though there is surveillance in place for CSF, ASF, and FMD, it is apparent that the funding is wholly inadequate to provide a high level of confidence that one of these trade-limiting FADs will be rapidly detected in time to make a difference. This is evidenced by the discontinuation in 2015 because of a lack of funding of a pilot project conducted by USDA's Veterinary Services, using the surveillance infrastructure built for CSF to actively detect ASF and FMD.

*Data sharing for regulated diseases.*—As evidenced during the HPAI outbreak, the amount of movement, testing, and premises data that needs to be captured, analyzed, and visualized by the APHIS incident command—responsible for dealing with animals disease outbreaks—to support disease response and business continuity activities is staggering. While the various pieces of this type of data exist, much of it resides in disparate databases that do not readily and easily communicate, which hinders the response and jeopardizes animal welfare. The industry is very concerned that this lack of connectivity will have direct and negative effects that will hinder the response to a foreign animal disease of swine.

CONCLUSION

There seems to be a growing consensus that there are serious flaws in the country's preparedness to deal with threats to U.S. agriculture and the U.S. food supply.

The *Bipartisan Report of the Blue Ribbon Study Panel on Biodefense,* co-chaired by former DHS Secretary Tom Ridge and former Sen. Joe Lieberman and released Oct. 28, 2015, highlighted the need for improvements in the system for protecting the U.S. livestock herd and the Nation's food supply. Concerns about the adequacy of the country's preparedness also were raised in a Nov. 4, 2015, hearing of the House Agriculture Committee.

NPPC urges Congress to use the information gathered in that hearing and in the Blue Ribbon Study Panel report to work with the Obama administration on finding solutions to improve the preparedness of the United States to deal with any pest or disease outbreak.

Ms. McSALLY. Thank you, Mr. Acord. The Chair now recognizes Dr. Williams for 5 minutes.

## STATEMENT OF BRIAN R. WILLIAMS, ASSISTANT EXTENSION PROFESSOR, MISSISSIPPI STATE UNIVERSITY

Mr. WILLIAMS. Chairman McSally and Members of the sub-committee, thank you for the opportunity to appear today to talk about the risk that our Nation faces from agroterrorism. As an ag economist from Mississippi State University, I spend a large portion of my time researching ag markets and the impacts that shocks can have to those markets. Our country's ag and food production system faces many challenges today, one of which is a risk of major disruption to the system. It is essential that we be prepared to face these threats to prevent and/or minimize the impacts they may have on our food system.

As mentioned by my fellow witnesses, our poultry industry faces devastating Avian influenza outbreak in 2015. In Iowa alone, 30 million layers were lost, and 1.5 million turkeys were lost, resulting in a direct impact of $658 million.

Other industries are also impacted. This is known as a multiplier effect, and that multiplier effect resulted in a total economic impact of $1.2 billion, and more than 8,000 jobs lost.

On a positive note, some of those losses in Iowa were partially offset with increases in sales in other States. Mississippi alone, ag producers in the State saw 40 percent year-over-year increase in sales. Keep in mind, those increased egg prices were also passed on to consumers. So there is a negative on that side as well.

Prior to the Avian influenza outbreak, the poultry industry already had several biosecurity measures put in place by companies such as Sanderson Farms and Tyson, who owned the birds and contract the producers to grow and raise those birds. The State and Federal agencies also helped to develop those guidelines.

Despite all of these measures that were already in place, the industry was not prepared for an outbreak when disasters strike. In the time since the outbreak, industry leaders, State agencies and Federal agencies have all come together to develop a plan to quickly and efficiently address future outbreaks. This can also be applied to agroterrorism and provides an excellent framework for other industry to work from.

One benefit of agriculture is that production is spread over a wide area. As a result, natural disasters and other disruptions are quite common, but typically have minimal impacts. For example, the snowstorm about a month ago that hit the States of Nebraska, Iowa, Colorado, and Kansas, all but shut down the meat-packing industry for nearly 2 days. Yet the markets didn't respond to that shock.

Another example, a similar snowstorm earlier this year in Texas and New Mexico, killed more than 30,000 dairy cows, and caused significant damage on a local level. Yet Nationally, the milk futures only increased for a week before returning to their previous levels.

One of the greatest threats from agroterrorism that we face is an introduction of something that could shut down our export industry. An example of this is in 2003 when had a BSE, a cow test positive for BSE in Washington State that shut down our export industry on our beef cattle. It took 7 years for exports to return back to the level that they were before that positive test of BSE. But despite that shutdown in exports, the cattle markets really were not impacted on a large scale.

Moving on to our crop industry. With fruits and vegetables, the biggest threat that we really face is something that can potentially harm us as humans: The introduction of E. Coli, or salmonella. Our fruits and vegetables are typically grown outdoors, in the ground, many of them very close to the ground so they are susceptible to contamination, whether it be natural from birds or introduced from terrorists. While there is a system in place to detect and track these introductions, there is still definitely room for improvement in that area.

Row crops are much less susceptible to agroterrorism and natural disasters. The damage must be on a large scale to have a significant impact on the Nation's economy. The biggest threat that we face right now is drought, a wide-spread drought as we saw in 2012. The 2012 drought took nearly 3 years for our Nation's row crop industry to really get back to normal levels.

The other thing to keep in mind on that side of things is the conditions have to be nearly perfect at the field level for a terrorist to introduce a pathogen that would really take hold and spread. So, the likelihood of that is not very high.

In conclusion, past incidences of disruption have shown the U.S. ag sector is remarkably resilient. In most cases, it would be difficult for a producer to inflict damage on a large enough scale, with the exception of possibly our foot-and-mouth disease, and some of these diseases in the livestock sector, to cause a National impact. What is really key to minimizing these effects is to take measures to keep them at a localized level. If these impacts are at a localized level, our ag sector has shown a remarkable ability to bounce back from these types of incidences.

[The prepared statement of Mr. Williams follows:]

PREPARED STATEMENT OF BRIAN R. WILLIAMS

FEBRUARY 26, 2016

Chairman Donovan and Members of the Emergency Preparedness, Response, and Communications Subcommittee, thank you for the opportunity to appear today to talk about the risk that our Nation faces from individuals or organizations who wish to disrupt our agricultural and food system. I am an agricultural economist from Mississippi State University and spend a large portion of my time researching agricultural markets and the impacts of various shocks to the markets. Our country's agricultural and food production system faces many challenges today, one of which is the risk of a major disruption to the system; whether it be in the form of a terrorist attack or from a natural disruption. It is essential that we be prepared to face these threats to prevent and/or minimize the impacts they may have on our food system.

LEARNING FROM RECENT EVENTS

In August of 2015, an outbreak of Highly Pathogenic Avian Influenza (HPAI) hit several States in the Midwest and Pacific Northwest, inflicting a significant amount of damage in its path. Iowa alone lost 30 million layers and pullets as well as 1.5 million turkeys with direct impact of just over $658 million (Iowa Farm Bureau, 2015). In addition to the direct impact of lost production, there are also indirect impacts that need to be considered. For example, suppliers and vendors that normally market goods and services to the poultry operations will see reduced income. As a result, they will make fewer household purchases, hurting the sales of additional businesses; creating a multiplier effect. According to a study commissioned by Iowa Farm Bureau, this multiplier effect resulted in a total economic impact of $1.2 billion to the State of Iowa's economy, including 8,444 lost jobs.

Agricultural production in the United States is dispersed across a large area, which helps to mitigate impacts on a National level. In the case of egg production, while Iowa saw significantly reduced production, other States saw increases in their sales. I have estimated that the State of Mississippi alone, egg producers benefited from an increase of $93.6 million in production, a 40 percent year-over-year increase, as a result of increased egg prices. It is highly likely that several other States experienced similar increases in egg sales. Of course, the increased egg prices are ultimately passed on to consumers, increasing the average American's grocery bill. This phenomenon is also pointed out by Pendell et al. in their study of the potential release of foot-and-mouth disease from the future National Bio and Agro Defense Facility in Manhattan, Kansas.

Much can be learned from the HPAI outbreak in the spring of 2015. Prior to the outbreak, the poultry industry already had several bio-security measures in place. Many of those measures had been put into place by companies such as Sanderson Farms and Tyson, who own the birds but are contracting producers to grow and raise them, as a protection for their investment. Many of the protocols already in place by the bird owners were developed with the assistant of State agencies. The USDA and APHIS also had several simple, commonsense guidelines in place. Despite all of these measures that were already in place, the industry was ill-prepared for actually dealing with a disastrous event such as HPAI. In the time since the outbreak in 2015, industry leaders, State agencies, and Federal agencies have all come together to develop an elaborate plan to quickly and efficiently address future outbreaks. The plan includes a quarantine of the infected area, testing of all birds within a 3-mile radius, and requiring a written permit for anyone entering and/or exiting the area. The model that the poultry industry has put into place can easily be applied even in the case of agro-terrorism and provides an excellent framework for other industries as well.

### ECONOMIC IMPACTS IN ANIMAL AGRICULTURE

There are several things to consider when trying to estimate the economic impact of a terrorist attack on animal agriculture. First, how wide-spread is the damage? If the damage is localized to a single county or even multi-county area, the impact will likely be minimal. In some cases, insurance will pay indemnities to producers for the value of the animals that are lost. Indemnities may also be paid by the USDA. If facilities must be quarantined or sterilized before introducing new animals, insurance will not reimburse producers for lost future production. That could compound the economic impact of a disease outbreak, whether natural or introduced by terrorists. As mentioned above, there are also multiplier effects that must be factored in. For example, in the State of Mississippi the multiplier effect for jobs is 2.32 (Henderson et al. 2015). In other words, for every job lost in the agricultural sector there are 1.32 additional jobs lost in the rest of the economy.

One benefit of agriculture is that production is spread over a wide area. As a result, natural disasters and other disruptions to production are quite common but typically have minimal impacts on the economy and markets. For example, the February 2, 2016 snowstorm that hit much of Nebraska and Iowa prevented many cattle from being transported from feedlots to packers and all but shut down the meat packing industry for 2 days, but the Fed Cattle markets did not deviate from their normal patterns. A similar early January snowstorm in Texas and New Mexico killed more than 30,000 dairy cows, and caused significant local damage. Market fundamentals tell us that when supply is decreased, prices should shift higher, yet milk futures only increased slightly and the higher prices lasted less than a week before declining again. The impact of the Texas snowstorm was only temporary because although the storm brought significant local damage, 30,000 head of dairy cattle is relatively small when compared to the more than 9.3 million head of dairy cattle in the entire United States.

One of the greatest threats from agro-terrorism that we face is the introduction of a disease or pathogen that causes our export markets to be shut down. We saw one such incident in 2003 when a cow from Washington State was found to be infected with BSE, shutting down the majority of our beef exports (See figures 1 and 2 below). It took over 7 years for U.S. beef exports to return to levels seen before the first BSE case was discovered. Despite a complete shutdown in U.S. beef exports that took several years to recover, cattle prices showed little-to-no impact as shown in figure 3 below.

### IMPACTS IN PLANT-BASED AGRICULTURE

Plant-based agriculture can be broken down into two general groups: Fruits and vegetables that are grown for direct human consumption and row crops that are typically grown for animal consumption or for additional processing that ultimately leads to human consumption. In the fruit and vegetable category, the biggest threat we face is the introduction of food-borne illnesses such as e-coli or salmonella. Leafy greens are of particular vulnerability due to their fragile nature that makes them difficult to clean as well as a consumer's tendency to eat them uncooked. Many fruits and vegetables are grown outdoors in the ground, where they are susceptible to contamination from natural sources such as birds, but are also easy to access by terrorists interested in introducing food-borne illnesses into the food system. While there is a system in place to detect, track, and recall contaminated foods, there is still room for improvement (Coates and Trounce, 2011).

Row crop agriculture may also be susceptible to agro-terrorism and natural disasters, however the damage must be on a wide scale to have a significant impact on the economy. The biggest threat to our row crops is a wide-spread drought such as the one experienced in 2012. As shown in figure 4, the 2011 drought that hit the Southern Plains and then the 2012 drought that swept through much of the Corn Belt and Southern Plains caused a substantial drop in corn production as well as a spike in corn prices. It took U.S. corn producers nearly 3 years to rebuild corn stocks to the point where markets have returned to a new equilibrium. The high grain prices caused by the 2011–2012 droughts were also responsible for the agricultural boom that the United States experienced in 2013 and into 2014. Farm incomes hit a record high in 2013, which provided a boost to other agricultural businesses, caused farmland values to rise, and boosted the economies in several rural States. While the impact of the 2012 drought help some in the agricultural industry, others were harmed. Higher corn prices drove up costs for livestock producers, the ethanol industry, and ultimately it drove up food prices for consumers. While unlikely, a terrorist attack that can reduce production any individual row crop could cause similar impacts as the 2012 drought. However, if harm is inflicted on only one crop I would expect markets to return to normal much more quickly than they did following a drought that impacts the production of not just one crop, but several.

In conclusion, upon examining past incidences of disruptions in production and trade across a variety of commodities, the U.S. agricultural sector has demonstrated a remarkable resilience. In most cases, it would be difficult for a terrorist to inflict damage on a large enough scale to have a lasting detrimental impact on the U.S. economy. If a terrorist were to succeed in inflicting damage on a large scale, the agricultural industry has proven that it can recover quickly from most threats. With the cooperation of individual industry groups, State governments, and the Federal Government in devising plans to respond to potential terror attacks or natural disasters, evidence suggests that damage from such disasters can be mitigated.

REFERENCES

Coates, A. and M. B. Trounce. "FDA Food Safety Modernization Act: Is it Enough?" Journal of Bioterrorism and Biodefense. 2:109. 2011.

Decision Innovative Solutions, "Economic Impact of Highly Pathogenic Avian Influenza on Poultry in Iowa." Prepared for Iowa Farm Bureau. August 17, 2015.

Henderson, James E., James N. Barnes, and Lawrence L. Falconer. "The Economic Contribution of Agriculture and Forestry Production and Processing in Mississippi." Mississippi State University Extension Service. Publication No. 2879.

Pendell, Dustin L., Thomas L. Marsh, Keith H. Coble, Jayson L. Lusk, and Sara C. Szmania. "Economic Assessment of FMDv Releases from the National Bio and Agro Defense Facility." PLoS ONE 10(6): June 2015.

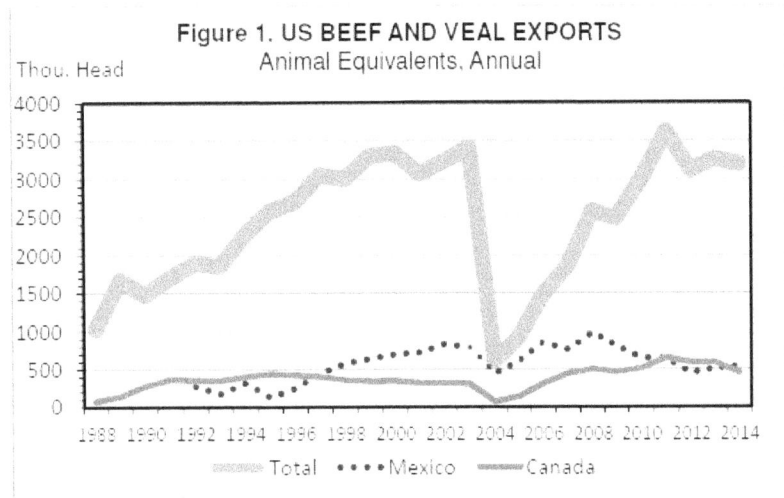

Figure 1. US BEEF AND VEAL EXPORTS
Animal Equivalents, Annual

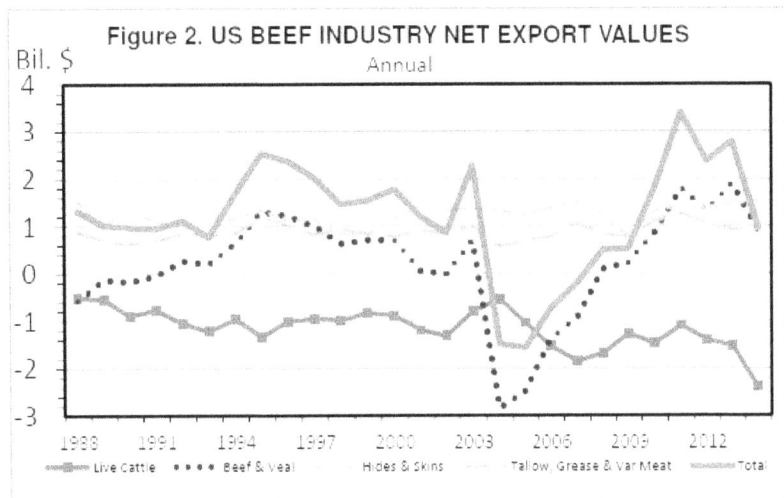

Figure 2. US BEEF INDUSTRY NET EXPORT VALUES
Annual

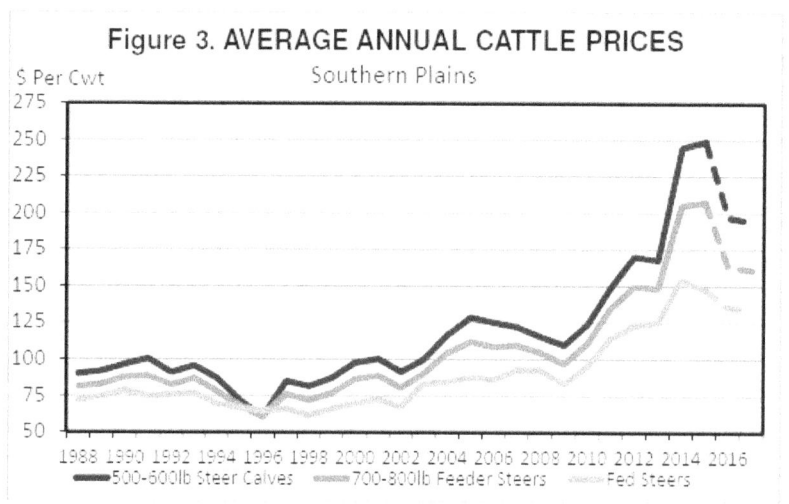

Figure 3. AVERAGE ANNUAL CATTLE PRICES

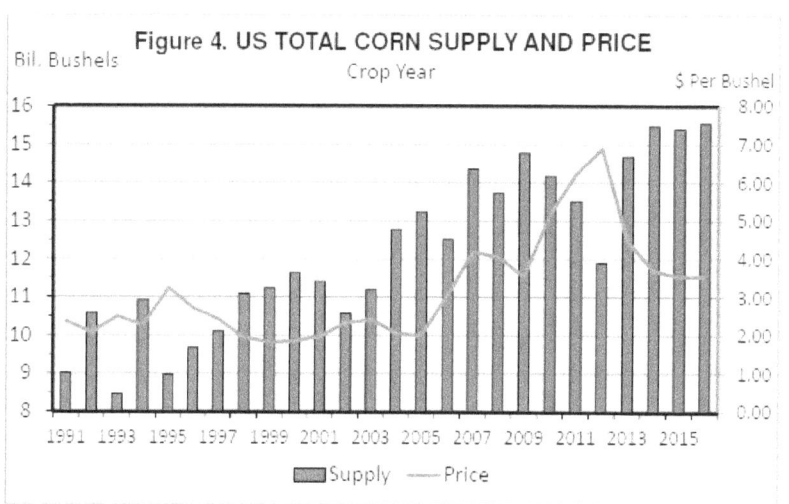

Figure 4. US TOTAL CORN SUPPLY AND PRICE

Ms. MCSALLY. Great, thank you, Dr. Williams. As Chair, I now recognize myself for 5 minutes for questions. A lot of them stewing here, but I want to be efficient with my time and give my colleagues the opportunity to ask questions.

This committee has very much been focusing on fusion centers and information sharing, not just between Federal partners, but between Federal, State, and local; not just on the Government side, but with private sector and others that would need a place, or maybe can be a place, regionally or State-wide, to come together and get the information that they need on threats and sharing information in both directions.

I would love to hear perspectives from any of the witnesses on whether you have been invited or involved in any of the fusion centers, or whether that is an area that we also need to be improve to be inviting members related to the agriculture industry to address the agroterrorism threat, to have that information be shared at the fusion centers.

Dr. MECKES. Chairman McSally, I will speak to our situation in North Carolina. As I indicated, the emergency programs division came into being in 2002, and they have been intimately involved with law enforcement, with our emergency management response teams all across the State of North Carolina with the fusion centers. Again, I would suggest that the emergency programs division model might be something that other States would consider, because it has taken the burden of trying to manage that piece of agriculture and food defense off of our veterinary division, in that this group focuses solely on what is needed for response. Of course, we are integrated with them on a day-to-day basis in all the activities. So yes, in answer to your question, North Carolina does have input and does receive input from the fusion centers and the emergency management.

Ms. MCSALLY. Is that all virtual, or do you have somebody who is invited there or sits there if something were to break out? Are there tactics, techniques, and procedures, TTPs, for you to have somebody there or how does that work?

Dr. MECKES. In our planning for high-pathogen influenza, we actively engaged immediately our emergency operations center for the State of North Carolina, and we would have run the incident out of that emergency operations center.

Ms. MCSALLY. Okay, great. Any other witnesses care to comment on the fusion center? Mr. Acord.

Mr. ACORD. To my knowledge, there has been no discussion or contact from those centers with the pork industry. I haven't heard of any.

I can make you aware of one circumstance where communication is not good, and that is with the National Animal Health Laboratory Network. The challenge that we have there is that most of the laboratories can't communicate with each other, and that is a serious, serious consequence of not being able to immediately post what you find in a laboratory in Minnesota, in Iowa, in Kansas, and that has to be fixed if we are going to have an effective system, and it currently doesn't work.

Ms. MCSALLY. Interesting. Dr. Beckham.

Dr. BECKHAM. That goes back to biosurveillance and having the ability for systems to communicate with each other to include the laboratory systems. As currently stands right now, the ability for those labs to message test results and communicate with one another, as Dr. Acord says, is not as robust as it could be. In addition, getting information from the field, from the veterinarians to the State animal health official, or to other officials who need to have that information, right now there is not a really robust system out there for that. There are some efforts underway that are all-of-enterprise efforts from the industry to the State animal health official, to the Federal Government that have been funded by the Department of Homeland Security and that are being coordinated with USDA to develop surveillance systems that ultimately can talk between each other in the diagnostic labs, but to date, obviously that is still underway, and that has not reached its full potential, much less even broached the idea of communicating with our public health sector.

Ms. MCSALLY. So, we had a hearing about 2 weeks ago taking a look at biosurveillance systems, and particularly, looking at the National Biosurveillance Integration Center. So is that a place where—I mean, there is a lot of shortfalls and shortcomings to that, but in Nirvana, in a perfect world, is that a place that should be integrating this information in a two-way, and across regionally as well?

Dr. BECKHAM. So I think there are some challenges associated with that. I think some of the challenges are the willingness to share information. Someone has to act as a trusted agent, which is kind of what I alluded to in my testimony. The industries, I believe, are willing to share information, but that information has to be protected, and there has to be clear policies and procedures on how one will react to certain types of information.

So those things need to be worked out, and, I think, you know, one of the projects that I had previously worked on in academia with industry was really headed that way so that you could get people to share information. But more importantly than getting them to share, you have to give them something back for it. They can't just give you information and you not give anything back.

So, it is a two-way street, there has to be good communication and there has to be trust, and I am not sure that NBAF is the place for that. I would let my other witnesses up here comment on that. I think Doug is ready to do that. But I can sure tell you that academia is a good place, or maybe another third party that can act as a trusted agent would be a great place to hold information, or to share information.

I will say one more thing, and the unique thing about some of the systems out there now is that you actually don't even have to hold the information, you can reach back to that information and gather that information and only use it when you need to use it; therefore, it stays with the owner, the actual owner of the information. So that is another way getting access to information and being able to utilize information, but not storing information in big databases, which can sometimes be very vicarious.

Ms. MCSALLY. When you were saying that, it made me think of a parallel that we had with a cybersecurity and information sharing among the private sector and with the Government, and we actually passed legislation out of this committee providing some protections to the private sector to build that trust in liability issues so that there could be sharing of what the appropriate threat information is. So I wonder if that is a model to look at for a similar challenge within this industry. I have some more questions but I am out of time. So I will go on a second round here. So I want to give some time to Ranking Member Payne for 5 minutes.

Mr. PAYNE. Thank you, Madam Chair.

This question is for all the witnesses. What is the biggest gap in our ability to prevent and mitigate the effects of an agroterrorism event? What is the most critical investment we can make to prevent such an event?

Dr. BECKHAM. Early detection, early detection is key, right? So we have got to know something is here. We have got to be able to localize it, keep it localized. So early detection, biosurveillance, the National Animal Health Laboratory Network, the investment on these laboratories, the investment of that infrastructure is absolutely critical.

You heard earlier today vaccines are an issue for foot-and-mouth disease. I will take that one step further: Look at the funding we put into HHS and the funding in the Strategic National Stockpile, and then compare that to what we put into the National Veterinary Stockpile. We do not have the funding to prepare this Nation to respond to with vaccines and diagnostics that we need. So I would say that is a large gap as well.

So for me, it is early detection and then the countermeasures to respond, but the funding has to be there similar to what we see on the human side of the house. We have a zoonotic disease incursion, we have got to have the capabilities to respond. In order to do that, we have to have the resources allocated before. We cannot be reactive, we have to be proactive.

Dr. MECKES. Just to provide an order of magnitude of the funding for the National Veterinary Stockpile, $1–2 million per year, contrast that to the strategic National stockpile, which is $3–4 billion a year. I suspect the strategic National stockpile throws away more drugs that are expired on an annual basis than the entire budget of the National veterinary stockpile. We have to begin to address that issue. Foot-and-mouth disease is the barbarians at the gate. It is just a matter of time before it is introduced into this country, and we cannot stop the spread of that disease.

Mr. ACORD. For the livestock industry, I think it would have to be an adequate supply of foot-and-mouth disease vaccine, that is really the thing that scares us the most. I agree with Dr. Beckham that early detection and rapid response is the mantra that we have to follow. But we know right now that we do not have an adequate supply of FMD vaccine, nor do we even have a vaccine for something like African swine fever that has spread rapidly through Russia and into eastern Europe. It is only a matter of time before it moves elsewhere. We have to address those things. We can't continue to talk about it. USDA puts in about $1.9 million into the vaccine bank. That is a pittance compared to the loss that we would suffer with a foot-and-mouth disease outbreak.

Mr. WILLIAMS. I would mirror what Dr. Beckham and Mr. Acord have said. The key is early detection and taking care of things as soon and as quickly as possible. The quicker that we stop the spread of any such disease, the less economic impact that we are going to have. So, that is, to me, really the key, is getting on top of this as quickly as possible and doing everything we can to have a response plan in place, whether its vaccination, or other measures, to really get on top of this and prevent it from spreading.

Mr. PAYNE. Thank you. Mr. Acord, in your testimony, you acknowledge that every passenger and handbag entering the United States has a potential to import a disease that could harm the agriculture industry. In your opinion, is the United States doing enough to keep diseases and pests out of the United States? What should be done—what more should be done?

Mr. ACORD. Well, I think the effort has improved dramatically to address this issue. We are looking at an almost impossible job when you—I have spent a lot of time at the Miami International Airport, and I take pork producers there all the time so that they can see what is intercepted at the Port of Miami. In a few days, in a few days, you have a mountain of intercepted material, and it is unbelievable what people want to bring in, and they have all kinds of opportunity to declare that they have something, but they don't. I saw one passenger from Venezuela was literally bringing a grocery store in a suitcase, and said they have nothing. Thank goodness for the dogs.

One of positive things that has happened, and I never thought I would say this at the time, but moving the agriculture inspectors to the Bureau of Customs and Border Protection was a very, very smart move. When I talked to those inspectors now, they tell me that the improved enforcement authority that they have through the Customs laws has contributed immensely to their ability to do their job. We have to spend more time at the country of origin, and the country of departure rather than the border. That is literally our second line of defense.

We are going to have to put more people in these countries if we expect to have any possibility of finding out what is going into these products in the first place that is, like I say, about the PED, however that got in, that same pathway is still open for FMD for which we have no vaccine. So we just have to direct more resources to country of origin, I think.

Mr. PAYNE. Thank you. Madam Chair, I yield back.

Ms. MCSALLY. Thank you, Ranking Member Payne. The Chair now recognizes Mr. Donovan from New York for 5 minutes.

Mr. DONOVAN. Thank you, Madam Chair. Mr. Acord, Mr. Payne, and I would like you to visit Newark International Airport as well, please, that is our airport.

Everyone here has spoken about early detection, and it is so multifaceted when you think about home-grown products and live-stock, imported products and livestock. How are we doing this early detection? First, maybe we could do it domestically. Are the people on the ground trained to detect, or do we wait until someone gets sick and then try and find out the origin of that illness? How is it that we are doing early detection? Certainly, if we are doing it, whatever methods we are using now, how can they be improved? I open that up to the panel.

Dr. MECKES. Member Donovan, I would suggest that that takes place at the State and local level. The State animal health officials, my team within the veterinary division that is on the ground every day with pork producers, with poultry producers, with beef and dairy producers, we are out there seeing animals, we are talking to the producers, we are working closely with private practitioners. That is where we will detect the disease. Rightly, that should be the case. We are in touch with everything that goes on in our respective States.

Dr. Beckham worked closely to develop a program 3 years ago called enhanced passive surveillance, which was a means of identifying diseases early in animal agricultural production. It was almost like emergency room visits that were recorded and tracked on a day-to-day basis.

So, we have to make sure that capability exists. I am going to suggest that DHS has a unique role in all of this, and, of course, I draw upon my 7 years in the Office of Health Affairs, but USDA has a significant regulatory responsibility. DHS has a significant threat reduction responsibility, and it should work to enhance capabilities all across the country in preparedness and response.

A perfect example of that would have been the Center for Domestic Preparedness in Anniston, Alabama. The Ag Earth program, the Ag Emergency Response Training Program. After 5 years of successful operation, FEMA discontinued funding for that program because it was perceived as a non-issue for our country.

Obviously, it remains an issue and will be an issue. So DHS should step up, and appropriately so, work on the threat side, work on the preparedness side, and work on the response side with States all over the country.

Mr. DONOVAN. Doctor.

Dr. BECKHAM. I would just echo what Dr. Meckes said, and say that, of the veterinarians we are training every day, and the colleges of veterinary medicine, and the ones that are out practicing, are really the first line of response.

Early detection is multifaceted, so it is heavily dependent on the producers recognizing there is something wrong, calling that veterinarian, getting them out there. Then through this system, that Dr. Meckes mentioned, we have the capability of collecting that information on multiple devices and bringing that in and having veterinarians have the capability to share that through multiple devices as well, so if they are seeing something that is unusual in one area, they can share it with each other and say: Hey, is anybody else seeing this?

Those are the kinds of systems we have to develop, and those are the kinds of systems we have to implement if we are going to have a comprehensive program for early detection that really relies on the first responders, the veterinarians, and the producers that then works with our State veterinarians to and get all that information back.

Mr. DONOVAN. Is it more difficult to detect a disease in our grown products, our agriculture products, than it is livestock? It sounds like, not that it is easy to detect with livestock, but it seems like there may be more signs.

Dr. BECKHAM. You will see clinical signs, right, exactly.

Mr. ACORD. I would agree with Dr. Beckham and Dr. Meckes. I think the private practitioner is the first person that is going to be the one to find a foreign animal disease in the United States.

The pork industry spends a great deal of time talking to our producers. We have educational material, that they were provided, that encourages them to report any unusual conditions, that they observe, to both their local veterinarian and subsequent to their veterinarian, to the State veterinarian.

We have a foreign animal disease diagnostic training program, at Plum Island Animal Disease Center, where foreign animal disease diagnosticians are trained to recognize the symptoms of disease. That certainly could be expanded to include a larger number of people because it is very unique training where they actually get to see the disease. These animals are infected with foot-and-mouth disease, so they can see first-hand the symptoms. I think we have a start, I guess that is how I would characterize it.

Mr. DONOVAN. My time is expired. I would like to, if we do a second round, ask you about how we do this detection for things that we import. But, Madam Chair, I yield the rest of my time, which isn't any.

Ms. MCSALLY. Thank you, Mr. Donovan. The Chair now recognizes Ms. Watson Coleman from New Jersey for 5 minutes.

Mrs. WATSON COLEMAN. Thank you very much. I have a number of questions which have been prompted from just listening in and out. We talked about detection, and we are talking about elimination, and we are talking about vaccines. I want to go before that. Are there standards that people who grow crops have to follow, people who grow livestock have to follow?

Are there standards to ensure that these products are being grown and these livestock are being bred and surviving under certain standards for safety? Is there such a thing, and if so, who is responsible for policing that or monitoring that? What is the process for that?

Dr. MECKES. Well, I will say first and foremost that the marketplace drives those standards. If you are a producer of pork, if you are a beef producer, if you are a dairyman producing milk every day, you want to meet those market standards to be assured that your product can go to market.

Mrs. WATSON COLEMAN. Yeah, that is taste and stuff. I am talking about are there standards that you can only grow in this kind of soil this? You have to do this in order to protect a plant that is growing. If it is livestock, it can only be bred under certain circumstances. They can only be fed under certain circumstances. Ways that you would prevent diseases and things of that nature, as opposed to waiting until something happens and then having the capacity to detect it. I just want to know if there is any such thing?

Mr. ACORD. Well, in the pork industry, we have the Pork Quality Assurance Program, which sets some standards that determine issues like animal welfare, animal health monitoring, those kind of things. That does exist, and there is a great deal of education of producers that goes into implementing that program.

Mrs. WATSON COLEMAN. Who monitors that that is actually happening? Are those Federal standards?

Mr. ACORD. No, ma'am. They are not Federal standards.

Mrs. WATSON COLEMAN. They are industry standards?

Mr. ACORD. They are industry standards. I would suggest to you that there would be a great reluctance, and an absolute opposition, by producers to be confined by any kind of Federal standards as to how they raise livestock and produce crops. I think the industry would view that as probably un-American, quite honestly, to see that.

Mrs. WATSON COLEMAN. Even if the goal is to make sure that livestock and veggies and whatever are produced in a healthy way so that you don't have these various diseases?

Mr. ACORD. I don't think you can regulate industry or production of anything to that extent. There aren't enough resources to monitor how that is done and, quite honestly, we can pass all kinds of regulations. It is the ability to enforce those regulations that makes a difference.

Mrs. WATSON COLEMAN. Yeah. I was kind of trying to get at that also. Are there standards? Who monitors? Should there be monitoring? You are saying that such a thing isn't very viable in the industry. I know that the producers would probably resist it, but I am just wondering, does Government have a role in that, and if so, what would it be?

I can go on to some other areas because—and I think it was you, Mr. Acord, I think you said that there is no FMD vaccine? Does that mean you have none stockpiled or that none exists because there is no vaccine? I don't know.

Mr. ACORD. Well, there is a limited availability of vaccine.

Mrs. WATSON COLEMAN. So there is a vaccine, but it is not available?

Mr. ACORD. At Plum Island Animal Disease Center is where the United States maintains its bank. That is the bank for North America. You know, Canada, Mexico, and United States, all would use it. The antigen is stored there because the law prohibits live FMD virus on the U.S. mainland. That antigen is shipped to Europe where it is manufactured into finished vaccine and shipped back to the United States, but it has such few strains. The problem with it is that the antigen has a shelf life.

Mrs. WATSON COLEMAN. That is what I was going to ask you. Does it have a shelf life?

Mr. ACORD. After 5 years, the potency of vaccine starts to go down, and after 10 years it is not all that effective quite honestly, and the companies don't even want to touch the manufacture at that point.

Mrs. WATSON COLEMAN. So one thing that I read, is that, there are so many entities and agencies involved in this whole discussion that we are having today, Madam Chairman, and I need to understand what would be the most efficient involvement of agencies and the most efficient collaboration that could take place that is information sharing and facilitated and not impeding and not delayed because there are just so many cooks in that pot.

I guess I will have to wait until the next round to hear the answer to that, but that certainly is something that I think we need to be exploring. Thank you very much.

Ms. McSALLY. Thank you. The gentle lady yields back. The Chair now recognizes Mr. Walker from North Carolina.

Mr. WALKER. Thank you, Madam Chairwoman. Insider threat, seems to be a significant danger. If there was an attack, would it be able to establish a chain of command? Is there any kind of protocol? Maybe, Dr. Beckham, would you touch on that, or Dr. Meckes, either one——

Dr. BECKHAM. I am going to let Dr. Meckes because they handle it at the State level typically.

Dr. MECKES. We follow the incident command structure to respond to any incident, whether it is a hurricane, a tornado. We have just spent the last 7 months preparing for the introduction of

High Path AI in North Carolina, which thankfully has not come to pass; but we developed our entire incident command structure to address every issue associated with an outbreak of High Path Avian Influenza.

Everything from burial and disposal to the movement of samples to the laboratory for testing, routing of vehicles to make certain that we can effectively continue to move product and maintain some continuity of business, even in the face of a disease outbreak. So FEMA's incident command structure is the hierarchy by which we will operate, and practically speaking, every Department of ag across the country is familiar at some level with this incident command structure.

Mr. WALKER. Being a little privileged to the North Carolina situation, being your home base, North Carolina is ranked at the top, or at least in the top 5, really in all areas of this emergency preparedness. I commend your work on behalf of doing your part in the agriculture side to keep it so highly ranked.

Dr. MECKES. Well, it hasn't been my work. It has been my predecessors'. I thankfully walked into a well-oiled machine to respond to incidents.

Mr. WALKER. Well as we have seen around here at the State level, you have to have good people to keep those machines going. Otherwise they can end abruptly.

Getting outside of North Carolina, are you familiar—does anybody want to address that—across the country, in our Agriculture Emergency Operations Center, are we seeing good capability across the country? Are we being followed as a model—can anybody address that?

Dr. MECKES. There is a spectrum of capability across the country, a wide spectrum. I think, again, that is where DHS has a role in working towards, with USDA—now when I say DHS, we always were diligent in making sure that we cooperated, cooperated, coordinated, and collaborated with our sister departments and agencies in addressing any of these issues. So we held a Foot-and-Mouth Disease outbreak with FEMA Region 7 in December 2013, and every player was at the table, the States, the locals, and DHS, and HHS for that matter.

So it has to be an integrated effort, but DHS does have a significant role and an important role in driving preparedness and response capability.

Mr. WALKER. I have a final question, but I am not so sure I want to ask it publicly. It may come back with you. Where it talks about America's food, agricultural sector, where is the most vulnerable target that we have to agroterrorism, but that may be a question better not shared publicly.

So with that I am going to I yield back the balance of my time, back to you, Madam Chairwoman.

Ms. MCSALLY. Thank you. The gentleman yields back. We will, I think, be voting soon, but I want to give an opportunity for second round here until votes are called. I appreciate the thoughtful questions and discussion so far.

One concern we have seen across many industries with the rise of terrorism, and ISIS, and the home-grown extremism, is the potential use of drones for some sort of attack, and it doesn't take much imagination to consider how, I mean, people are getting these for Christmas, and they are much cheaper and easier to buy now, how that could be used in such a way to deliver something to a crop or to a farm to have an agroterrorism attack.

Is that something that is even being looked at, at all by any of you, and any ideas and considerations for addressing this difficult threat?

Mr. ACORD. While it is an additional potential for introduction of disease, I don't see it creating anything new, because agriculture is so open. Animal production is so open. There is access to farmland and to barns rather easily, so I don't think that is going to pose anything additional in terms of worry for the agriculture industry.

Dr. MECKES. Chairwoman, I will share with you that during the past virus outbreak which began in April 2013, and arrived in North Carolina shortly thereafter, that our colleagues in the environmental realm used drones to surveil disposal of piglets that had died all throughout eastern North Carolina, so that was a concern.

We obviously did our best to make certain that we didn't create an environmental problem associated with an agricultural disease outbreak, but who knows where this goes in the future. It may well be a concern.

Ms. MCSALLY. I mean, they can be used positively as well obviously for surveillance.

One question, Dr. Beckham. I have a lot of friends who are veterinarians, so this is more anecdotal, both small animal and large animal, but one thing they share is there are fewer and fewer people that are choosing that field of work. It is becoming more and more expensive. They are going, like a lot of higher education, but they are going significantly into debt, and so it is a bit of a deterrent to even choose the field. So part of making sure that we are ready in this area is making sure that we have the next generation being trained up.

I know at the University of Arizona anyway, they are trying to do a bit of an innovative program to compress the number of years for the Bachelor's and moving on from there, and also something innovative that would impact rural communities where an individual would graduate as a Doctor of Veterinary Medicine, but also have a Nurse Practitioner license so that the human-animal bridge could be addressed in some of these rural areas. I think some of those innovations would actually help in this area as well.

Are there any other innovative ideas out there? I think that is an interesting model perhaps. Are you concerned about the pipeline and training of the next generation?

Dr. BECKHAM. So I am incredibly concerned about it, which is actually why I went to Kansas State University to be the dean there. I think it is something as a profession we have to address. We are producing about 80 percent small animal veterinarians for a variety of reasons, and we are losing the expertise that is going back to detect the work in the livestock systems and production animal medicine. There is a whole host of reasons why that is happening.

We as a profession have to come together and look at novel, innovative ways to get students in and out with less student loan debt. We have to give them additional skill sets, like you mentioned the nurse practitioner. We at Kansas State University pride ourselves on the fact that we still have one of the locations that produce quite a bit of students that go out into production animal medicine. We have a rural veterinary loan program where we will pay tuition for those that agree to go back into Kansas and work in rural areas. We have to continue to look at novel, innovative ways to do that.

So we are starting to look at that as well; how do you compress the time it takes a student to get in and then get out; are there ways that we can do it more efficiently, and those types of things. But we as a profession have to take a look at that across the United States. That is something I think we are starting to do, but I don't know that we have done that aggressively enough.

Ms. McSALLY. I encourage you to take a look at what they are doing from the bottom up, you know, groundbreaking, at the University of Arizona, because it seems likes it is pretty innovative. Where a program doesn't exist, it is easier to create an innovative one as opposed to trying to change a program, so that kind of sharing best practices I think would help.

I know we are going to vote, so I yield back the balance of my time, and I will recognize Mr. Payne for another 5 minutes.

Mr. PAYNE. Thank you, Madam Chair. Mr. Williams, you mentioned biosecurity measures developed by the poultry industry following the Avian Flu outbreak and how the model developed by the poultry industry can be applied across various agriculture industries. Can you elaborate on the best way for the public and the private sectors to help drive participation and adopt biosecurity measures that are mutually beneficial to each other?

Mr. WILLIAMS. Well, just to kind of talk a little bit more about what I have seen in the State of Mississippi. After the Avian Influenza outbreak a year ago, producers were incredibly concerned and so they were very willing to come to the table and to work with the State veterinarian, to work with the USDA, to work with APHIS, in developing these plans.

I think really what it comes down to is we need a boots-on-the-ground approach. These producers that we were talking to, that we were discussing this with over the summer, we were giving them signs to look for. That is something that our veterinarians can really help with, is not only with poultry, but with beef cattle, with the pork industry, tell them and inform them, what do we need to look for, for signs of a potential outbreak? Then when you see these signs, when you see these symptoms, report them immediately to your State veterinarian, to your local veterinarian, and have it investigated.

We were even talking about backyard birds, backyard poultry farmers, or backyard poultry operations, if you see something, report it immediately. That is really the system that they have started to get in place to recognize things as quickly as we possibly can, to get on top of it, to quarantine the area, and to localize it as much as possible.

Mr. PAYNE. So if you see something, say something, right?

Mr. WILLIAMS. Exactly.

Mr. ACORD. May I comment, sir?

Mr. PAYNE. Sure.

Mr. ACORD. The pork industry has always prided itself on having a very good biosecurity system. That is because of the structure of the industry, we know that we are more vulnerable to disease. But at the same time, while we thought we had the perfect system, when we had the PED outbreak, we discovered a lot of holes in that system, and we have begun working on those.

The other point I want to make, and it hasn't been brought up here, is we have a huge threat from urban animal agriculture. It is unbelievable how much poultry, even now into potbelly pigs, to sheep and goats in some places are kept in urban environments. They totally escape the animal health network, and are the most vulnerable to disease introduction, and that is an area that we have to start paying much more attention to than we have up to this point.

We have had problems with live bird markets in New York and places like that, but that is nothing compared to what we saw in Los Angeles when we had exotic Newcastle disease in poultry there. So that is another vulnerability that we haven't looked at hard enough.

Mr. PAYNE. Thank you. Dr. Beckham, it is my understanding that Kansas State partnered with FEMA to develop an animal disease outbreak training course. Can you describe how KSU is working with FEMA to push out this training opportunity?

Dr. BECKHAM. I think that falls under the Biosecurity Research Institute, where they are actually using that facility to train veterinarians on signs and clinical symptoms for foreign animal diseases, and so it is a novel use of that facility to be able to bring veterinarians in and provide that kind of training there in Kansas, so it is really unique, and it aligns closely obviously with what happens at the Plum Island Animal Disease Center.

So the more we can do those kinds of things outside of containment in Plum Island and demonstrate those types of diseases and whether it is using plasticized material or tissues to do that, that is at least one component of training a cadre of veterinarians that can go out there and do that. There are many of those foreign animal disease diagnostic practitioner courses that happen at Colorado State as well. So they also happen other places in the United States, so there is the FADD course, the Foreign Animal Disease Diagnostician course at Plum Island; and then there is other courses that happen around the United States, at K State, at Colorado State, that use different technologies to teach the same type of information.

Mr. PAYNE. Thank you. Madam Chair, I yield back.

Ms. MCSALLY. Thank you. The Chair now recognizes Mr. Donovan from New York.

Mr. DONOVAN. We are being told votes are going to be in about 2 minutes, so let me just ask the question I wanted to ask in the first round. We spoke about domestic protection. Since we import so many products, where is our importation detection? Where are we making the detections internationally for products being brought into the country?

Mr. ACORD. I can speak from the Animal and Plant Health Inspection Service standpoint that a risk assessment is done anytime there is a request to import or to export a commodity from another country to the United States. They are asked to provide a lot of information about the existence of disease within their country. What kind of surveillance do they have, do they have competent authority, do they have enough veterinarians to deal with disease? Those kind of fundamental questions. Sometimes it results in a site visit, most often actually it is a site visit to go look at the country and see if what they are telling the United States is true, and then there is a formal risk assessment that is done.

But there are a lot of products, that are getting into this country, that are not getting the kind of review in country that they need from the standpoint of the manufacture of those products. So we have a gap in that area and not enough is being done. We cannot rely on the port of entry as being the first line of defense. That is not going to work. We have proven that.

Mr. DONOVAN. You are speaking about cooperative countries. If something is introduced into our imported foods purposefully, all the help, with the exporting country, isn't going to help, so are we doing any detection methods for products coming in aside from relying on the exporting country, that you are aware of?

Dr. MECKES. There is a group within DHS that, as Bobby mentioned, reviews product shipping invoices on a day-to-day basis and inspects those that have the greatest risk or the greatest perceived risk. But that being said, less than 2 percent of all products imported in the United States are physically inspected in any form or fashion.

So Mr. Donovan, you are correct, that someone with less than stellar intent could intentionally bring something into this country that would never be physically observed.

Mr. DONOVAN. Maybe as my colleague, Mark Walker said, maybe we shouldn't have said that publicly. Madam Chair, I think that was the roll call. I will waive the remainder of my time.

Ms. MCSALLY. Okay. Great, Mr. Donovan. The gentleman yields back.

Just in closing, in my time in the military, we always would talk about threat equals capability plus intent. Clearly we have heard today from our witnesses the capabilities are there. We do also know that the intent is there for potential agroterrorism attack.

We do know, I was looking back at my notes, in 2002 we had a Navy SEAL team raid al-Qaeda storehouse caves in Afghanistan, finding documents how to carry out a terror attack on America's agriculture. As you mentioned, Dr. Beckham, these types of agents naturally exist in places controlled by ISIS, Boko Haram, al-Shabab, and others. I quote former Secretary of Health and Human Services, Tommy Thompson, when he, in his farewell address, when he left in 2004, which is 12 years ago, he said: "For the life of me I cannot understand why the terrorists have not targeted our food supply, because it is so easy to do." Again, we hold this hearing not to instill fear in the American public, but to raise awareness on what the threats are, what the capabilities are, and what the intent is, and identify what we can do as a Federal Government, but working closely with the private sector, States, local authorities, and academia in order to address these vulnerabilities and these threats in order to keep our country, our food supply, our agricultural system, safe and secure from these types of threats.

That was a great hearing, and I appreciate all the witnesses' testimony today.

I do want to say, closing out my final hearing here, you are all in good hands. I am handing over the gavel to Mr. Donovan. It has been a pleasure to be chairing the subcommittee. I enjoyed working with Ranking Member Payne. Again, I will be remaining on the subcommittee, but we will continue to move forward on some of these really pressing issues.

I want to thank all the witness for their expertise in this area and your hard work and your testimony today. The Members of the subcommittee may have some additional questions for the witnesses. We will ask that you respond to these in writing. Pursuant to Committee Rule 7(e), the hearing record will be open for 10 days.

Without objection, the subcommittee stands adjourned.

[Whereupon, at 11:34 a.m., the subcommittee was adjourned.]

○

www.ingramcontent.com/pod-product-compliance
Lightning Source LLC
Chambersburg PA
CBHW081751280526
45789CB00008B/2819